Baird T. Spalding
...AS I KNEW HIM

BY
David Bruton

DeVORSS & CO., *Publishers*
P.O. Box 550
Marina del Rey, CA 90294

DEDICATION

This book is dedicated to the vast number of people whose lives have been transformed by the writings of Baird T. Spalding. Its aim is to present Spalding as a human being, which he claimed to be, not as a god, to which he made no claims. It is my hope the following pages will give additional insight into this famous man's life and thereby endear him to you for his true worth. As in the case of every individual, his true worth was founded in him as he was, not as others dreamed him to be. In this spirit, I offer you, his friends and admirers,

BAIRD T. SPALDING *As I Knew Him*

TABLE OF CONTENTS

Preface 5

Chapter I
THE LINE OF DESTINY........................... 13

Chapter II
MEETING BAIRD T. SPALDING 21

Chapter III
THE SPALDING LECTURES....................... 41

Chapter IV
THE FABULOUS BAIRD T. SPALDING 55

Chapter V
SPALDING'S DEATH.............................. 75

Chapter VI
BAIRD T. SPALDING AFTER DEATH 91

CONCLUSION 102

PUBLISHER'S PREFACE

To the Second Edition

Over the many years that we have published *The Life and Teaching of the Masters of the Far East*, we have received innumerable inquiries and requests for information about Baird T. Spalding and his India Expedition upon which the books are based. Although we knew of the existence of David Bruton's book, it was out of print, and we felt there was no way we could verify Mr. Bruton's statements; nor could the contents of the book be summarized in brief form so as to give an adequate picture of the entire situation.

It is with some trepidation that we venture to publish a second edition of this astonishing little book, which has been out of print for many years. In addition to dispelling the "Spalding myth," Mr. Bruton said some very uncomplimentary things about Douglas DeVorss, the founder of our publishing company. We feel, however, that the fact that Mr. DeVorss had human failings should not, at this point, interfere with what Mr. Bruton was trying to accomplish with his book—to answer questions and resolve the mystery about the Spalding books, and to put them in a truthful historical perspective.

In the almost fifty years since the first Spalding volume was published, the letters that have come from readers can leave no doubt that the books have been of inestimable value to a great many people in their search for faith and meaning. The basic ideas presented are in harmony with the ancient wisdom teachings found throughout the classics of metaphysical literature; and in the final analysis, therein lies the value of these books.

We believe that Mr. Bruton's account is sincere. How much it was colored by his own personality and perception, we do not know; nor is it possible for us to verify his "facts." The story has elements of humor and mystery, and a good share of constructive and instructive philosophy that students of metaphysics, and followers of "gurus" would do well to consider with care and mindfulness.

As Mr. Bruton states: "Were he (Spalding) expanded to meet the most fanciful dreams of his, he would have been, at best, a conveyor of a message. He was not the message itself. One would not think of showering adoration on a Western Union boy at the sacrifice of the message he was delivering! Jesus taught, 'I of myself am nothing . . .' and directed attention to the Principle within."

DeVorss & Company

Arthur R. Peattie, President
Hedda G. Lark, Editor

March 15, 1980

PREFACE

The major part of this manuscript was prepared shortly after the transition of Baird T. Spalding; in fact, I started it on March 30, 1953. Much of the material is taken from notes made over a period of years; some information was given to me expressly for this writing.

In a way, I feel a responsibility to both Mr. Spalding and his reading public for issuing a realistic picture of him. I have received a volume of correspondence from Spalding readers which indicates, as a whole, they knew very little of his life. News of his death was not widespread and, consequently, only a comparative few are aware of his passing.

Spalding skyrocketed to phenomenal fame almost overnight. Despite the fact that his books were never promoted, they swept him into a position where his readers regarded him as an authority on religious matters. As his books traveled from country to country, he gained more momentum in this respect for, in the main, he was accepted totally.

PREFACE

The whole story of Baird T. Spalding is fantastic from beginning to end. In releasing the manuscript for his First Volume he carved a unique niche in life for himself that probably will not be duplicated or repeated by another individual this century. The book which gave him international publicity was really incidental to him. He preferred to be known as a "Research Engineer," not as author, philosopher or religionist. His chief interest in life was mining which occupied most of his time.

Spalding's admirers assigned to him certain attributes and evolutionary attainments to which he made no claim. From his writings, the popular conception became rather fixed that his alleged association with the Masters had achieved at least a degree of Mastership for him. However, Spalding states he was one of a "research party" who visited the Far East. Three of the party stayed to devote their lives to the teaching of the Masters but he was not one of them. There is a vast difference between going on a visit to the Far East and becoming an earnest follower of the Masters' instruction.

One of the amazing things about Spalding's life was the intense feeling generated for him by hundreds of thousands who knew him only through the printed page. When news of his death arrived in Los Angeles, people who had never seen him were grief stricken. One lady remained in a state of hysteria for over two weeks; others refused to believe it was possible for Spalding to die. Some staunch devotees admitted he might pass through death but contended he would probably resurrect himself as a young man within a few days. One couple traveled from Los Angeles to Tempe, Arizona to attend Spalding's funeral because they were firmly convinced he would turn to Light at the last moment.

We who were rather close to Spalding watched him fail in health over a period of months. It was evident he suffered a heart condition. Except for the surprise that always attends announcement of death, none of us were upset, and certainly not disillusioned, because Spalding died.

Soon after I returned from Spalding's funeral in Arizona I spoke to Douglas K. DeVorss, publisher of the Spalding books and my first book, about writing a story on Spalding's life. DeVorss discouraged the idea. When I mentioned to him in May, 1953, that I had the manuscript almost finished, he did not care to read it. Confronted with this attitude, I decided I had overrated the importance of such a work and laid it aside. However, with Mr. DeVorss' sudden death in September, 1953, I became the sole survivor in possession of certain information regarding Spalding and in a singular position to pass it on or not.

DeVorss was apparently apprehensive about what I might say in presenting an intimate glimpse of Spalding. I think he felt if a long standing illusion which surrounded Spalding were shattered, book sales would drop. DeVorss did not hesitate to uphold the Spalding illusion when it seemed fitting to do so. This is evidenced in the dittoed copy announcement of Spalding's death. Only a few hundred of these were sent out. A. K. Mozumdar and Baird T. Spalding shared the same page. Mozumdar had twice the space of that given to Spalding: It read:

"DURING THE PAST WEEK, TWO OF OUR MOST PROMINENT AND DISTINGUISHED CLIENTS HAVE MADE THEIR TRANSITION FROM THE PHYSICAL FORM. SINCE IT IS NOT POSSIBLE TO WRITE INDIVIDUAL LETTERS TO ALL PERSONS INTERESTED, WE ARE TAKING THIS METHOD OF GIVING YOU THE FACTS.

A. K. MOZUMDAR

.   .   .   .

BAIRD T. SPALDING

"Baird T. Spalding, 95, research engineer, world traveler and author of the four volumes entitled 'Life and

8

Teaching of the Masters of the Far East,' died March 17, 1953 in Tempe, Arizona.

"Mr. Spalding was known internationally to more than a million readers of his books and had lectured in more than 200 American cities.

"Funeral services were conducted by David Bruton, Sunday, March 22, at 3 P.M. at the Carr Mortuary, Tempe, Arizona.

"Mr. Spalding was enroute from his mining properties in New Mexico to Los Angeles at the time of his death in a Tempe hotel.

DOUGLAS K. DEVORSS"

Some of the "facts" were not facts at all; they were actually misleading. If you received one of these copies and want the facts, which are a matter of record, please make the following corrections:

Mr. Spalding died March 18, 1953 instead of March 17. He was not enroute from his mining properties in New Mexico. He owned no mining properties. His name appeared on a number of claims.

Mr. Spalding was not on his way to Los Angeles and had no intention of going there. He was enroute to Reno, Nevada. He planned to return to New Mexico from Nevada.

His death did not occur in a Tempe hotel; it was a Tempe motel.

I offer documentary verification of my statements in this book.

Considering these few alterations of "facts," the picture is slightly changed. The DeVorss statement might easily convey an impression that Mr. Spalding had extensive mining properties since he was a "research engineer, world traveler and author." One would probably visualize Spalding traveling by train and stopping in the best hotels, a picture commensurate with his holdings. Certainly, one would never guess Spalding was really traveling in a 1947 truck, dressed as a typical miner, with only $15.98 in his pockets when he died.

DeVorss knew Spalding was enroute to Reno, Nevada because a letter from Spalding asking DeVorss to mail his monthly check there was received by DeVorss on March 17.

I wish to state clearly that I was not a follower of Baird T. Spalding and, contrary to reports, I was never a pupil of his. He had no pupils. I did not cling to every word Spalding uttered nor did I accept it as law, or even true, because he said it. This remark may seem harsh to those who did not know him, but, to his personal friends, it will be appreciated and understood. My meaning is not to be misconstrued for I was genuinely fond of Baird T. Spalding.

Although I marvelled at him in many ways, I personally considered him to be more fabulous than great. He fulfilled a great destiny in a fabulous way. I cannot conscientiously extol his work for any premeditated humanitarian effect. I can, however, praise him generously for what it accomplished.

David Bruton
Rolling Hills, California

May 26, 1954

THE LINE OF DESTINY

Chapter One

The life story of Baird Spalding presented a fluctuating gamut of extremes. Happiness came to him spasmodically while tragedy lingered in the background of his mind to drive him relentlessly toward further accomplishment. In a sense, he rode the crest of the wave of success while, at the same time, he was filled with the despair of failure. He was rejected and eulogized, ridiculed and revered, damned and deified as the hour-glass of destiny slowly poured its sands along his Path.

No living person could write an accurate biography of Baird Thomas Spalding unless the information were taken directly from the Akashic Records. Scarcely anything is known of his early life except what he related of it. On two different occasions I asked him where he was born. The first time he told me in "upstate New York;" the second, "Spalding, England." During one of his last public lectures a member of the audience asked where he was born and he answered, "In India."· He spoke with equal affection for the "old family home" in upstate New York, in Spalding, England and in Coconada, Madras Prov-

ince, India.   Knowing Spalding, as I did, would not war-
rant any attempt on my part to do his life story from
readily available facts.   I merely recount incidents that
occurred during my relationship with him and as told by
others to me.

The Spalding line of destiny crossed my path when I
read his first book.   Although I lived in a small mid-
western town, a copy of his First Volume reached me
soon after its release.   I was sixteen years old; however,
I was not a new student of occult studies.   My childhood
training was under the vigilance of a High Initiate who
acquainted me with esoteric work little known in America.
At that time, I had no direct contact with a Master but I
did possess a knowledge of Their lives and work.

My reaction to Spalding's book was similar to that of
most people inasmuch as I wanted to know, beyond doubt,
whether or not these writings were true.   I have since
learned that many people are inspired to go to India and
experience for themselves the things which Spalding related.   This urge was not as strong in me as my determina-
tion to meet the author and ask him countless questions.

I did not doubt the power of the Masters in command-
ing the elements, as Spalding stated.   My doubt was that
Spalding had seen the feats performed which he reported.

Above all, I could not understand why the Masters would so willingly display Their "wares" to scientists who were, obviously, disinterested in the philosophic or religious trend of Their work. From my knowledge of Them, such behaviour was unlikely.

The Spalding book was a sharp departure from current reading of the day. Marie Corelli's novels were based on experiences with the Masters but she classified her writings as fiction. A few groups were teaching of the Masters; notably, the Theosophical Society. Their work was not founded on personal contact with Them but presented from an academic viewpoint. The world of science had made no attempt to study the lives of the Masters; hence, most of the knowledge about Them was derived from philosophy and fiction.

The first copies of Spalding's book stated in the "Foreword" that he, Spalding, was a member of a group of scientists sponsored by a well-known American university which was specifically commissioned to do research on the Masters of the Far East. The first Spalding book was published as a report of their findings. The university soon put an end to the use of its name and emphatically denied that Spalding was ever a member of their staff. Only a comparative few of these original copies were ever circulated. My copy was such an original. Now, the

Baird T. Spalding As I Knew Him

"Foreword" states that Spalding was one of a research party who visited the Far East in 1894. It carefully says that he was an "independent" member of the party. All copies issued now are "Revised Editions" and different than the originals.

Because of the supposed scientific authority on which the Spalding book rested, many intellectuals accepted this "report" with open minds. A university graduate gave the book to me. His entire family considered it a substantially verified report.

Because of my deep-seated interest I vowed I would meet the author of this book someday and he would tell me directly whether or not it was a true account of his true experience.

During the past two years many people have secretly confessed to me that their feeling about the Spalding books were comparable to my own. Most of them had not been persistent enough to meet and know him. As a rule, his books had produced a very desirable effect on their lives and they were content to let the question rest.

Meeting Baird Spalding never became a particular campaign with me. I did think it important that I eventually talk with him but I refused to spend much time in seeking any individual or proving or disproving a way of life.

I spent much of my spare time studying various trends of thought and was always interested in groups which professed knowledge of the Masters. I attended all types of meetings merely to observe what was being taught. I did not enter into their activities or search in groups for my own enlightenment. Early in my youth I knew I would teach later on and this was the means I employed to acquaint myself with a cross-section of learning.

My musical training began when I was five years old. As a major pursuit, I followed this line of activity through high school and college. After college, I went to New York City to further my studies. While music absorbed most of my time, philosophy held my deepest interest. By the time I reached my twenties I knew many of the most prominent religious and philosophic leaders of the country. In our conversations, Spalding's name was frequently mentioned.

Most of the people with whom I talked regarding Spalding were of the opinion he spent most of his time in India. It seemed logical to me that he would become devoted to the Masters' Way of Life and follow Their teaching wholeheartedly; therefore, I did not push any questioning of him beyond casual conversation.

I came to California about the same time Spalding's Third Volume was published. He had been on a lecture tour and received quite a little newspaper publicity. Further than learning he had just returned from India I was unable to gain any more information about him. There was no choice but to postpone a concerted effort to meet him.

A few years later, while visiting a prominent Southern California lady who studied Metaphysics, the conversation drifted to Spalding. She had recently read his books and was anxious to discuss them. She told me of a friend who had spent an evening talking with Baird Spalding and considered it one of the highlights of her life. I learned he was frequently in Los Angeles; at least, he was expected to be there in the fall.

With my interest aroused, I wrote to him in care of his publisher. I received no answer and the letter was not returned. Six months later, I wrote a second letter; again, no answer and no return.

In the course of events, my attention was drawn to a small group which conducted closed meetings on the teachings of the Masters. The meetings were held on Sundays in a farmhouse near Los Angeles. I decided to "crash" one of these meetings, if possible. I asked a friend, Bill Hann, to accompany me. Bill was enthusiastic about the idea for he was curious in regard to this particular group and its teaching, too. Bill was more than curious about Spalding and we had often discussed his books and the possibility of meeting him.

Early one Sunday morning in the spring of 1950, Bill Hann and I headed for the farmhouse meeting. We arrived about an hour before the service was scheduled for there was the matter of talking our way in. The farm itself was not very impressive but the people gathered there were well-dressed and educated.

We located the leader and asked if we might attend their service. He was a tall, thin man who was evidently in ill health. He had a cautious air about him which I could understand because he was trying to figure us out and out-figure us at the same time.

He answered my plea for admission with a question, "Do you live every minute of your waking hours to the best of your ability?"

I recognized my answer held the key to my worthiness

and was honor bound to be truthful. Inwardly, I was highly amused and could hardly refrain from laughing.

I whipped back a short reply, "No, do you?"

This caught him off guard. Before he managed an answer, a devotee stepped to his side and whispered something to him. He excused himself and went inside. Just before the meeting began he came to the door and motioned Bill and me to join them.

The highly secret meeting turned out to be a cheap imitation of spiritualism. "Jehovah," no less, spoke. Bill was definitely not impressed and was ready to start home but, instead, we accepted an invitation for noon dinner. Afterward, I felt obligated to carry on some kind of conversation with the leader, and, besides, I did want to find out why they taught as they did. Bill spotted a lawn swing and went outside for a nap. I made myself comfortable for a long chat with the leader.

After listening about four hours to highly improbable and mysterious tales of the "Masters," I attempted to switch the subject by innocently asking my usual question.

"By the way, do you know Baird T. Spalding?"

"Why, I've known Baird for thirty years," came an unhurried answer.

MEETING BAIRD T. SPALDING

CHAPTER Two

The chill of the late afternoon air had prompted Bill to move inside. We were in the dining room. Bill, at one end of the long table, had scattered himself rather unevenly over the surface of a large club chair where he had remained in a semi-conscious state for some time. When our host calmly announced he had known Spalding for thirty years the sleep suddenly left Bill's eyes, he adjusted himself and leaned forward in his chair. I suppose I reacted almost as sharply because we were closing in on a desirable subject.

"Tell us something about Spalding," I urged, trying to get things in motion.

The man recognized our eagerness to hear of Spalding. He had been unsuccessful to this point in arresting more than a fragment of my wandering attention. I noticed a fleeting look of satisfaction pass over his face and wondered what was in store for us now.

"What do you want to know?" he asked, very graciously.

Baird T. Spalding As I Knew Him

"How old is he?"

"No one knows. He could be 75, 85 or almost 100."

"How old does he look?" I continued

"About fifty," he replied.

It was a little too much like playing a game. I knew he was just as anxious to tell us everything he knew about Spalding as we were to hear it. I assumed a more indifferent attitude and waited for any information he cared to give us.

"I haven't seen Baird for three or four years. He used to come up here quite a lot. Even his publisher doesn't know where he is. Says he has royalty checks piled up knee deep for Baird but doesn't know where to mail them."

Doesn't Mr. Spalding have a home?" I asked.

"No, he is a very free soul. Lives all over the world. He may be in Los Angeles one day, next week in South America, then show up in England, Italy or South Africa. No one can keep track of him."

"Does Mr. Spalding have an outstanding personality or is there anything unusual about him?" I asked.

Meeting Baird T. Spalding

This did it. No longer able to restrain himself, our host volunteered information running along these lines:

He said that Baird Spalding was the most unusual person he had ever known and that he had an unfathomable mind. Spalding, according to this man, had endless energy. He never knew what it meant to be tired. He told us of one time when he was moving his household goods across a canyon. There was no road and no way to move the furnishings except to carry them down one side of the canyon and up the other. Spalding happened along while the moving was in full swing and offered his services. Our informant said they could load Spalding like a pack mule and he would virtually run down one bank and up the other. None of the other movers could make more than two or three trips a day. Spalding made ten; at that, he showed no signs of fatigue.

He related to us many other Spalding incidents. One concerned a gathering of friends in a private home where an unexpected young man dropped in. Spalding hurried over to greet him soon after he arrived. He called the youth by name, asked about his parents and grandparents and made many remarks which showed an intimate knowledge of the boy's family. When the young man said he did not know Spalding, everyone was surprised. Spalding attempted to refresh his young friend's memory by mentioning his grandfather who operated the first grist mill in a certain section of Montana, the round-up given on the boy's eleventh birthday when a cowboy was thrown from a horse and broke his arm and other incidents.

The young man admitted he knew everyone who attended the round-up to which Spalding referred but there was no one by the name of Spalding present. He swore he had never met Baird Spalding.

The three of us speculated on how this may have been done by Spalding. Frankly, our guesses were not very valuable and not worth recording. Our host claimed he was present when the above scene occurred.

Next, he told this one, as nearly as I can recall his exact words:

"Some friends of mine asked Baird, along with other house guests, to spend a week with them at their beach home. Naturally, the refrigerator was filled with food when the guests arrived. The strange thing is that the refrigerator remained filled for the entire week without anyone going to the market. At the beginning of the week there was only enough food on hand for a couple of days. At the end of the week, after all had eaten, the same amount of food was still there. This was due to some kind of a law Baird was working."

I could not resist the comment, "I'd like to take him home with me for a while."

Perhaps Bill and I were too absorbed in the tales of Spalding. Something switched the trend of conversation from favorable reports to happenings which might depreciate our estimation of him.

"You know, Spalding was never in India until the 1935 tour."

"No, I didn't know that," I replied. "What was the source of his writings, then?"

"I don't know. I think he made them up as he went along. He wrote the Third Volume in my apartment in Los Angeles."

"How long did you say you have known him?" I questioned.

"Thirty years."

Baird T. Spalding *As I Knew Him*

"That would be from about 1920," I observed. "The material for Spalding's books were supposed to have been experienced around 1894 which was a quarter of a century before you met him."

Later, I was told the Third Volume had not been written in Los Angeles at all. DeVorss said it was written in the cabin of the late Dr. Mesik near San Diego. I had also been informed, by sources supposedly reliable, that some people had met Spalding in India before 1900. My tendency was to reserve any opinion on our host's remarks until I could establish more tangible evidence of Spalding's travels.

My attitude irritated our host but we worked over the hard spot and continued the conversation. Several remarks indicated he intended to discredit Spalding in our eyes.

"Take for example," he continued, "the time Baird was at my place and his attorney called. He wanted Baird to come to his office right away. Baird said he would. As soon as he hung up the phone, Baird turned to me and said, 'Can you let me have a dime for carfare down town?' I asked him what was wrong with the idea of putting out his hand and letting the money present itself like he spoke of in his books.

He said he hadn't time to discuss that right now."

Here he stopped, leaving Spalding in an unfavorable light. I saw an opening ahead.

"What did you do about Spalding's carfare?" I asked.

"O, I gave it to him, of course," he answered.

"Then it does work just as Spalding says. If you put out your hand the necessary amount of money will appear in it to take care of immediate needs," I exclaimed humorously.

Although he did not care for my brand of wit, my remark did serve to settle our talking into a more serious vein. He then told us many stories which illustrated Spalding's remarkable memory and wove a picture of him through his tales of travel and wide acquaintance.

He said Spalding had tapped a never-ending spring of knowledge and that he was a fascinating person to know.

Bill and I parted friends with our genial host.

Baird T. Spalding *As I Knew Him*

On our homeward trip, we thoroughly hashed over events of the day. The only impressive thing about our trek was the news of Spalding. Was he nothing more than a fraud? Did he derive some insatiable pleasure from duping masses of humanity? One minute we would wonder if he had played a cruel joke on everyone who was stupid enough to read his books; but the next, were unable to find a purpose for such a colossal hoax. Personally, I felt more muddled about Spalding now than at any time since I had heard of him.

In the following days and weeks I sifted every word I could recall of the eventful Sunday in an effort to get the bugs out of it. My interest in Spalding stepped up tremendously as the "plot" thickened. Now, I felt I had to meet him. I was convinced no intermediary would be able to convey an indefinite something about Spalding which I would discover in meeting him myself. If our Sunday on the farm had accomplished nothing more, Spalding was now a living, human being; he was a down-to-earth person like anyone else — yet something more.

I had exhausted every available avenue to meet Baird Spalding. If his publisher did not know his whereabouts, there was little chance I could find him. I alerted several people to keep an eye out for Spalding and asked them to let me know when he came to Los Angeles. Some of the lookout squad would eventually find him so I again relaxed my search.

The Spalding Fourth Volume had gained popularity in a group of my acquaintances. We discussed it frequently. It was decided I should teach the work to them but the plan failed to materialize. However, I did spend many hours explaining and clarifying this book to various gatherings and friends.

In August, 1950, I agreed to give a series of six talks in Fontana, California. These talks were to cover the main points of philosophy and give a skeletal working knowledge of the subject. This was in line with my current teaching and was not influenced in any way by Spalding. It was arranged by friends to have the talks recorded. Though I had no particular interest in the recordings at the time, they proved to be the link to my eventual meeting with Spalding.

When the series of talks was finished, Jul, my wife, and I left on a trip through the middle west. We sold our home, put the furniture in storage and planned to relocate somewhere along the trails of our journey. The rain and humidity of Arkansas and Missouri recalled to our minds the beautiful skies of Arizona. We headed back out west and arrived in Prescott, Arizona to pick up our mail on September 28. Four days later, we bought a log house in the pines and decided to stay.

In January, 1951, I received a typewritten transcript of the lectures which had been recorded in Fontana the previous summer. A short note requested that I put the talks into book form and have them published. I prepared a manuscript and went to Los Angeles to find a publisher. On my arrival, I submitted the manuscript to DeVorss and Company. It was accepted. The result is my first book, *The Unknown God Revealed*. At that time, it did not occur to me that DeVorss & Company also published the Spalding books.

Douglas K. DeVorss, my publisher, suggested I fill numerous speaking engagements in connection with the release of my book. I returned to Prescott, sold our house and Jul and I started back to California. We arrived in Los Angeles on July 1.

In the following weeks, while Jul handled the details of making speaking arrangements, I saw much of Doug DeVorss. One day while talking with him, I suddenly realized that he published the Spalding books.

Meeting Baird T. Spalding

"What ever became of Baird T. Spalding?" I asked.

"O, he's around town someplace," came a casual reply.

"That's one person I would like to meet," I ventured cautiously.

"You'll bump into him one of these days," was my unsatisfactory answer.

During the next two or three weeks I spent a great deal of time "just missing" Spalding. He would be in DeVorss' office one day and I would be in the next. Or, he would come in during the morning and I would be there in the afternoon. It was odd, but I became so accustomed to this routine that I instinctively knew when Spalding would be at DeVorss' office but I could never arrange to "accidentally" drop in at that time. I often remarked to DeVorss that I knew Spalding had been there at a certain time. He had been, too.

Frequent conferences between DeVorss and Spalding were necessary at this time because DeVorss was arranging a series of lectures for Spalding. Thirteen years had elapsed since Spalding had appeared before the public. Countless people were waiting to hear him again. Since I, too, met with DeVorss almost daily, I began to realize that meeting Spalding was really just a matter of bumping into him. I knew that if I put pressure on DeVorss for this long awaited introduction, he would probably become cagey and I would miss out entirely. Thousands of people would have hounded the publisher's office if they thought a glimpse of Spalding might be their reward. Some safeguard had to be taken.

Hundreds of letters came each month addressed to Spalding in care of the publisher. Spalding had given DeVorss permission to open them and he seldom read any of his mail. Lots of it could not be read anyway for it came from all countries of the world and De-Vorss did not employ interpreters. Some of the Spalding correspondence was answered by form letters, some of it was answered on the one day a month Mrs. DeVorss set aside for that purpose and most of it was never acknowledged. Spalding had no staff of his own, not even a secretary. I learned later that he carried on an extensive correspondence and typed his own letters.

My meeting with Spalding drifted along for two or three weeks. It was beginning to look as if I would never bump into him. One day, DeVorss and I were more or less idly talking when Doug said, "David, why don't you teach a class in Spalding's Fourth Volume?"

My day had arrived. I was quick to seize the opportunity. "I'd like to," I answered, "but it would be necessary for me to meet Spalding first. After all, it might be a little embarrassing if someone of my group asked if I knew Spalding and I had to confess I did not."

A case of this kind had just come up a few weeks previously. The teacher had never met Spalding and an old friend of Spalding's attended class. The pupil took over the class to such an extent that the teacher willfully quit. Therefore, I knew my request was reasonable.

"O, sure, sure. That's easy enough," came an affable reply. "I'll tell Mr. Spalding the next time he is in and we will set a definite date."

As simple as that — and I had struggled all these years!

The date was set. I remember it was a Tuesday morning at eleven o'clock. Yes, I was sure I could be there.

Jul and I were staying in Fontana at the time. Tuesday morning arrived and we donned our best for the Los Angeles trip. Neither Jul nor I knew just what to wear for although we had been told Mr. Spalding was a very plain man that could mean almost anything. Maybe he was someone who said, "Hi, Joe," when he met you but was dressed like the president of the bank or, another type who said, "Hi, Joe" when he met you and you felt you were in.

We arrived in Los Angeles early enough but did not make our appearance at DeVorss' office until one minute before eleven. No Spalding. DeVorss had no more than assured us, "He'll be along in a minute," when on the dot of eleven the door opened and there was our man.

I was so surprised! He was a little short fellow only five feet six inches tall. Had he been six feet five, I could have easily accepted him. I had seen pictures of Spalding and I knew he was not very tall. He must have impressed me as a "big man" because of my prolonged interest in meeting him.

Spalding wore a tan tweed sport coat, brown slacks, felt hat and highly polished shoes. His coat was the typical "shopping" variety; not too well pressed but not unkempt.

DeVorss had told me Spalding suffered an atomic radiation burn which affected the left side of his nose. At the time we met him, his nose was very irritated and bothered him noticeably.

Baird T. Spalding was quiet and unassuming. When we exchanged greetings he was almost shy. He did not appear ill at ease; rather, he was hesitant to push himself into the picture. One thing which may have caused him to retract into his shell was the fact that he had an appointment to meet people about lectures and teaching. Had the meeting been on a different theme I think he would have responded in a different way. He was not overjoyed at the thought of public lectures and certainly not burning with desire for me to teach his book. He was probably unsure of himself because he did not know what he was getting into.

I was really surprised at Jul's reaction to Baird Spalding. It was a case of love at first sight. From the moment Spalding walked through the door that Tuesday morning in DeVorss' office, Jul carried an affection for him that I have seldom seen her display. This attitude prevailed until the end.

Mr. Spalding sat across from me and general conversation started. DeVorss explained the idea he had in mind about lectures and my teaching the Fourth Volume. I sensed Spalding felt he should become a little better acquainted before he committed himself with me. I, in turn, left the initiative to him and conversed just enough that my presence was not forgotten. I asked Spalding no direct questions. When he addressed me he always looked at DeVorss. Jul was less inhibited and hopped right into the talk. I noticed Spalding did not hesitate to look at her when he answered. He apparently thought I had some kind of a proposition or "deal" up my sleeve and if he kept real quiet it might drop out before he was too involved.

The subject of dogs arose. Mr. Spalding spoke so affectionately of the leader of his Alaskan dog team. No one thinks more of dogs than Jul. For the next thirty minutes I thought I had been derailed in my purpose. Finally, my turn came. Spalding mentioned something of his project.

"What project is that, Mr. Spalding?" I asked.

"My Time Camera," he replied.

"I haven't heard anything about it. What do you mean?"

Spalding loosened up and began telling me of a camera on which he and others were working. He said it would photograph back through time and pick up actual scenes and sounds of historical events. Both Steinmetz and Edison thought this could be done. Not that it mattered, but I thought so, too.

"I can see two major problems in such an invention, Mr. Spalding. First, to find the rate of vibration of the individual which would lead to the event and second, to hold the vibration and slow it down to a speed where it could be photographed."

"Yes," he agreed, "those are the problems. But with the electronic microscope we have been greatly aided in overcoming these factors . . . . . "

With this, he became technical and explained some of the process by which it is possible to photograph back through time. And, incidentally, he was looking at me now. I felt he had at last said, "Hi, Joe" and I was in.

We continued our friendly chat until after noon.

Baird T. Spalding As I Knew Him

Mr. DeVorss was genuinely relieved to see Jul, Spalding and me hitting it off so well. For some reason, DeVorss was hesitant to let Spalding and me get together. Perhaps it was because I had so freely tangled with another of his authors when he tried to convert me on a few points of philosophy. This happened in DeVorss' office and Doug wanted Spalding spared. I liked Baird Spalding from the instant I first saw him and there was no real danger I would "put him on the fire."

DeVorss gave Spalding the benefit of the doubt in meeting the public. He was considerate of Spalding and careful in presenting people to him. As I was to learn, everyone had a tendency to take Spalding over. They wanted to get him out of the crowd, take him home with them, pump him endlessly for information and generally drain his energies if possible. This sort of thing was of no value to Spalding; it merely took his time and often interfered with other things he was doing. Doug managed Spalding for eighteen years. During this time he learned to apply necessary precautionary measures in Spalding's behalf. He was so kind and generous with his time he could never say "no" to anyone even though a request might be unreasonable.

Meeting Baird T. Spalding

Spalding loved people and loved to be with them. He did not care for crowds and always seemed to be in the act of adjusting to them. His favorite pastime was an evening with friends where he excelled in the almost extinct art of "visiting."

Spalding liked to spend much of his time alone. He knew where there were isolated shacks in desolate regions all over the west. He often went to one of these places where he could do just as he pleased. Only a few people knew he kept a solitude in such lonely spots for this information was strictly "top secret."

While Spalding was a talkative person once he started, he was extremely silent unless he wanted to talk. He said what he wanted to say because he wanted to say it.

He never defended his statements. If he thought anyone wanted him to make certain remarks, he would invariably dodge them. DeVorss accepted this and never suggested a topic for his talks. There was no choice but to leave him to his own devices.

Not much was said of the proposed lectures and teaching that first morning we met. It was just as well, for another time was set to talk over business. Jul and I were happy for the experience and we felt we had all been "old friends."

THE SPALDING LECTURES

CHAPTER THREE

Other meetings with Mr. Spalding were arranged and on each occasion he was more affable. The novelty of knowing him quickly disappeared. It was a mystery to me why I should have had such a different attitude in meeting this man, anyway. Now, as I look back, I marvel at it all the more for he was certainly not the first famous person I ever met. Always before, though, I had taken them in my stride.

I wanted Spalding to begin his talks in Fontana or somewhere in that vicinity. I knew many people there who wished to meet him and I felt his appearance in Fontana would probably be their only opportunity to do so. Location made little difference to Spalding followers for they would drive a hundred miles or more to hear him.

DeVorss thought Fontana was a good idea, too. Because Spalding had not appeared in public for so many years, a small place would give him a chance to get the feel of an audience again. Preparation for speeches never seemed to bother Spalding for, as far as anyone knew, he just started talking.

I arranged five consecutive nights for Mr. Spalding to speak at the Fontana Woman's Club, beginning on Monday night. My three day class on Spalding's Fourth Volume was scheduled to start Thursday afternoon.

Fumbling by DeVorss in publicity was responsible for poor attendance at these meetings. There were no newspaper announcements and mailed publicity was not delivered until a week after the lectures were finished. Even at that, people came from San Diego, Santa Monica, Long Beach, Hollywood and many other far off places.

Spalding was obviously a little nervous the first evening he spoke. After his lecture, I walked from the stage entrance to the front of the building with him, where he was to autograph books. On the way, I asked, "Did you have stage fright after such a long absence from audiences?"

"Why, no!" retorted Spalding as though such a thing were impossible. I was surprised at his answer but, later, I found that he had no sympathy for physical weakness in himself or anyone else. He would have considered stage fright a horrible weakness; besides, I had no business asking such a question.

I usually stood with Mr. Spalding while he autographed books and talked to members of his audience. It was necessary for someone to do this for there were, among his listeners, those who came to ridicule and criticize him. Not that Spalding was unable to hold his own in these matters but it was just not the object of the meetings. For instance, when Spalding was touring the East, a woman approached him after his talk and said, "Mr. Spalding, I think you are the biggest liar I ever heard." Spalding calmly replied, "Madame, everyone is entitled to his own opinion." When I sensed unpleasant situations, it was my duty to get the people moving. Often, one person would monopolize Mr. Spalding's time and thereby prevent other people from meeting him.

It was interesting to me to be with Spalding in this manner. I heard all conversations between him and those whom he met. It gave me a keen insight into his mind in a very short time.

While we were still in Fontana, a lady said to Spalding, "Of course, you do not remember me, Mr. Spalding . . ." He interrupted, "My dear Mrs. (calling her by name,) I should say I do remember you. You spent a week-end with us in Long Beach . . . " and fluently recalled incidents of that time. The lady turned to me in utter amazement, "Why, that was twenty years ago," she said. "I haven't seen him since!"

Baird T. Spalding As I Knew Him

I was soon convinced there was no end to Spalding's ready knowledge. I heard him repeatedly come up with the right answers on almost any topic, any place or any time. His memory feats were more than phenomenal; they were fantastic and unbelievable. Somehow, one feels in a position to deal with phenomena for there is a pre-supposition that it can be explained. It was different with Spalding. Just about the time one thought he had found the answer to his mind an unpredicted angle would appear which destroyed the theory. This was not my experience alone; it was a bewilderment everyone shared who knew him. His uncanny answers were always easy, usually obvious and, as a rule, the only answer which would fit that particular question.

He had the smoothest way of evading a question he did not intend to answer of anyone I ever encountered. He not only employed the usual tricks of not hearing or understanding the question but he could convert the idea into something he was willing to discuss. This usually confused his interrogator by upsetting his train of thought and Spalding could answer anything and get away with it. Contrary to an observer's opinion, it did not mean Spalding was incapable of answering the question. He never skirted a mental tussle; however, he did like the arena to operate on his own terms. I do not mean he displayed pride in his mental capabilities. He was kind and patient and seemed to derive no pleasure from belittling another's point of view.

At one lecture, a group of university science students attended to heckle Spalding. During the questions and answers period which followed his talks, they asked Spalding technical questions that required exact scientific knowledge to answer. Spalding gave simple answers for the convenience of his audience until the questions became too complicated to be handled that way. He then explained, and in detail, the precise scientific procedure which closed the discussion. After the meeting, the students came to him in open admiration for his genius.

Nothing quite so interesting happened that first week in Fontana. His audience was appreciative for the opportunity of hearing him and his appearances were successful.

Wednesday night, Mr. Spalding informed me that he intended to come to my class the following day. His interests were widespread and I am sure he was more than curious about my teaching of his book. Spalding was not at all pleased with the Fourth Volume for he insisted he did not write it. Technically, this is true. The Fourth Volume was taken from talks Spalding gave on the boat when he and his party made the India tour. The talks

were taken in shorthand and sent to DeVorss. Some of
the ideas are poorly presented while some of them bear
the influence of one or more persons who edited the notes.
I pointed the inconsistencies out to DeVorss and told him
it was hazardous to attempt to follow this book as a text.
Without gaining Spalding's consent, DeVorss asked me if
I would edit the Fourth Volume again which I refused to
do. I felt the responsibility rested with Spalding for any
writing which bore his name as author.

The class assembled with the star pupil in attendance.
Out of courtesy, I asked Mr. Spalding to share the teaching
with me. His part of the work was limited to a few personal experiences he related to the group. He gave no
additional information on the teaching of the book. I am
the only person to have ever taught Baird T. Spalding from
his own writing. The situation delighted Mr. Spalding.
We have a tape recording of this two-hour class which is
highly prized.

Spalding study groups had sprung up all over the
country. Requests for a teacher of this material poured
into DeVorss & Company. Both DeVorss and Spalding
urged me to continue teaching his work. However, it was
not my desire to carry on the Spalding teaching since I had
work of my own to do.

THE SPALDING LECTURES

During the time I worked with Baird Spalding, under DeVorss' management, the highlight of the day came after the crowd went home. We were usually invited out for the rest of the evening and Spalding was in his glory with unhurried conversation. Our "evenings" often extended themselves into the near daylight hours. We discussed almost everything.

After Spalding was launched in his lectures, DeVorss decided to take over my management. About that time, Angela Morgan came along and the West Coast Lecture Bureau was revived. Baird T. Spalding, Angela Morgan and I were the lecturers. Doug and Dot DeVorss handled complete management for us. This was anything but a lucrative enterprise so far as I was concerned. Neither Angela or Baird came out as well as I did for they stayed with DeVorss longer. They sustained about the same rate of loss over a period of time and I severed connections within a matter of weeks. My termination with the West Coast Lecture Bureau came when I received a statement for my activities during the month of May, 1952. In one week I had spoken seven times to packed houses and owed DeVorss almost one hundred dollars. Spalding and Miss Morgan had different arrangements with the Bureau than mine but, by that, I do not mean they were better — just different. Spalding quit a short time after I did and Miss Morgan a little later than Spalding. The West Coast

Lecture Bureau folded up and all concerned breathed a sigh of relief.

Keeping an eye on Spalding at public talks was a full time job. He did not like the idea of someone managing him. If he had resisted anything done in his behalf, one would have had a clue to his thinking. As it was, he ignored the fact that anyone was concerned about him or his decisions of the moment.

Acting for Spalding, I accepted a tea engagement after one of his evening meetings. When we were ready to leave the auditorium, Spalding was not to be found. Just then, Jul came running into the building and breathlessly announced that Spalding was leaving in a car with people she did not know. We hurried to the parking lot and caught him. I called, "Mr. Spalding, have you forgotten we have an invitation for tea this evening?" His reply was of the nature that put both his new-found friends and us at ease but there was nothing to do but invite the whole group to go with us. At the tea, DeVorss rearranged Spalding's transportation and drove him back to Los Angeles himself.

We learned that the strangers had offered to take him home and, with his inability to say "no," there was no choice for him but to go. It was a distance of 75 miles.

While Spalding was unmanageable, in a sense, he

48

was absolutely dependable in regard to public appearances. DeVorss never worried that he might be late or fail to keep a speaking date. In the eighteen years DeVorss managed Spalding there were only two times Spalding failed to come through as expected. Once, Spalding was speaking at 2:00 o'clock in the afternoon. Some eager fans took him to lunch and assured him his engagement was for 2:30. At 2:20, Spalding arrived at the hall. DeVorss had been chattering about almost everything by this time trying to convince himself and the audience that Spalding would soon be there.

The other incident happened during the summer of 1952. Spalding was scheduled to speak three evenings in Long Beach, California. In the afternoon, on the day of his first talk, DeVorss received a telegram sent by Spalding from Texas. It said he had been in a flash flood, his car washed off the road and that his leg was hurt. He did not state the extent of his injuries, gave no address or say whether or not he was on his way to California. Spalding was a habitual victim of flash floods which meant anything could happen to him in one of them. DeVorss spent the rest of the afternoon on long distance telephone calling every hospital in the area where Spalding's wire originated. He did not locate him.

DeVorss was in quite a spot. I had left the West Coast

Lecture Bureau and was not available to pinch hit for Spalding. Angela Morgan was still with the Bureau and was not engaged that evening. Her recitals were refined and presented with the dignity that becomes a great artist. There was nothing sensational about them and, therefore, would not appeal to many of the Spalding audience. The genius of DeVorss came forth to solve the problem. He asked Angela to give several of her poems and then rounded up a glass eating "swami" who had recently descended on Hollywood. The "swami" was, undoubtedly, enlisted to keep Hindu wonders before the public and associated with Spalding while, at the same time, giving credence to Spalding assertions. "Swami" ate carpet tacks, drank cyanide and chewed on glass tumblers. I witnessed him stand before a microphone and crunch glass the first Saturday night he was in town. The Hollywood crowd has been on and off the hook so many times with Hindu spiritual leaders that even the amplifying system did not produce the proper horror of what they saw. The attitude of a relaxed audience was well stated by a Jewish lady who sat in the row behind me — "So vat? De guy eats glass!" Anyway, with this weird combination of Angela Morgan and the tack swallowing Hindu, the evening was a miserable flop. This was the last scheduled appearance of Baird T. Spalding. DeVorss cancelled the two remaining nights. Spalding made no effort to contact DeVorss until he "limped" into DeVorss' office about two weeks later. I was present when he arrived. Later, I learned he was not in a flash flood at all.

During the time I was associated with Baird Spalding, two incidents occurred which stand out in my mind. They are so typically Spalding. Once, a young college student asked if Spalding could tell him where he could find a rare chemical formula used in photographic developing. Spalding said, "I can give that to you. If you'd like to write it down, use my pen."

The student turned to me on completion of Spalding's dictation and said, "That's the right one, alright. I had it once before but lost it." Then, bewildered, he added, "But there are very few people who know this formula even exists!"

The other incident came about in this manner:

After another Spalding lecture, a middle-aged man intercepted him saying, "Mr. X (prominent speaker) says you were never in Tibet."

"Yes, I know," answered Spalding.

"Then how do you account for the fact he can make this statement if it isn't true?" continued the disgruntled gentleman.

Spalding, poised and calm, answered, "Mr. X was not with me."

Further conversation being useless, the man left.

Before I attended any of Spalding's lectures I was very curious about the material he would use for talks. Apparently, there was little more he could tell of the Masters of the Far East or he would have released it in book form. His reading public surrounded him with a fantastic glamour which he, apparently, felt obligated to uphold. Starting, as he did, at the top of the ladder by talking with Jesus and other Masters, he established an "unusual" reputation, to say the least. He was almost forced to incubate ideas that were off the beaten path and be prepared to protect them from general destruction. His line of defense was buried in the fact that scientific equipment and money to promote his projects were in India. His last year of talks served a dual purpose; namely, to make a comeback where interest had slipped in his behalf and to put in his bid for new laurels.

Spalding read on a wide range of subjects, but especially, along the lines of science-fiction; he had an excellent memory and a heavily charged imagination. He pulled vigorously on his natural assets in his conjuncture of the "time camera." He spoke at length on the various pictures they had obtained; among them, the signing of the Declaration of Independence, the Inauguration of Washington, the Inauguration of Truman and the Sermon on the Mount. In the "Sermon on the Mount" picture, a detail slipped by Spalding which proved his undoing. I shall disclose this later in the book.

Baird Spalding gave an interview to a feature writer of a Los Angeles newspaper which had as a central theme the "cloud walkers" he had witnessed in India. The article appeared with artist's sketch and stirred no little comment. He discussed the "cloud walkers" in some of his talks. That was really pathetic but went over, nevertheless, with a surprising number of people. I was tempted to ask Baird what these evolved souls did on a clear day. They would probably have to stay home. He used discretion sparingly when he was out to make an impression.

In the last of his talks he ran out of anything to say. Anything spectacular, that is. As a result, he stood before his audience and read from one of his three volumes until the whole room squirmed with restlessness. Once, before he began reading, a listener asked him something of the merit of wearing glasses. He emphatically spoke against them and gave the impression it showed a weakness in one's consciousness to be so afflicted. At the close of his lengthy dissertation, he absentmindedly put on his old horn-rimmed glasses and began to read. He interrupted himself, took off his glasses and said a few more words against wearing them, put them back on and finished his reading. Most of his audience was not amused but highly indignant.

In short, the Spalding lectures did not amount to much. He redeemed himself on his questions and answers period. When DeVorss broke him into the lecture platform, Spalding talked fifteen minutes and answered questions for forty-five minutes. Gradually, the lecture consumed forty-five minutes and his time devoted to questions dwindled to fifteen minutes. It is my opinion that the original idea was the better one.

THE FABULOUS BAIRD T. SPALDING

Chapter Four

Baird Thomas Spalding was unlike any person I have ever known. One could not be around him very long without realizing he was a walking contradiction. It was a constant source of amusement to watch him, listen to him and predict, if possible, what he might do next. During the past thirty years he has undoubtedly created for himself the most fantastic background of any person to have lived thus far in the twentieth century.

Many of the tales enveloping Spalding are conflicting. Some of them have the quality of being impossible; however, in so many instances, the impossible part of them is to disprove them. The imagination of enthusiastic Spalding admirers bestowed on him the fantasy he enjoyed. I never heard him deny a statement which gave him outstanding credit nor soft-pedal a flattering remark. Some of his personal letters I read as Administrator of his estate indicated he enjoyed, completely, all attention directed to him.

Whenever Spalding talked, he sounded as if he were telling a tall story. This, alone, put him in a class by himself because those who dedicate their lives to Higher Learning usually speak with well defined conviction. His "tales" were pleasant to hear and he related them in such a matter-of-fact way that one was apt to develop a guilt complex if he did not believe them.

It should be remembered that it is my intention to present a picture of Spalding as he was; this is a factual account of the man as I knew him. To me, he ceased to be a legendary figure the day we met which released me to study him realistically. I believe my views on Spalding are unbiased and I know they are without emotion. In gathering the material for this book I talked with scores of persons who knew Spalding. I can honestly say that no one of them held an unprejudiced or impersonal concept of him. Either they condemned him because of his shortcomings or gave him unjustifiable praise. Those who knew him intimately will appreciate my efforts in this writing and share with me a certain delight in knowing his true value. Nothing I could say would lessen the affection of his friends for him. This is the way I want it to be.

In the following, I cite an example of what I mean by saying some of the Spalding statements were impossible, fantastic and conflicting. The subject is his age.

On Spalding's birthday, May 26, 1952, we had a birthday

cake for him at DeVorss' office in downtown Los Angeles. On that date, he announced to the few of us present, that he was celebrating his 95th birthday. However, one man who had known Spalding a number of years told me he and Spalding were the same age — 60. Other close friends of Spalding said when he reached the age of 70, he added two years to his age for each following birthday. Instead of his being 96 in 1953, he would have been only 83, if the method of calculating is correct. The "Foreword" in his Volume One has a signed statement in regard to the writing dated "December 24, 1894." This lends support to the age of 95 at the time of his death for it is reasonable to assume he was 35 to 40 years old when this trip was taken. DeVorss told me he had talked with people in Chicago who declared they knew Spalding as a student at Calcutta University before the turn of the century and he was then about thirty years old. Again, 95 seems his probable age at death. An irate Spalding friend called me by telephone after his death and screamed, "What do you mean by permitting Mr. Spalding's age to be listed as 95 when you know very well he is 98?"

Shortly after I attended Spalding's 95th birthday party, he told friends of mine he would be 97 his next birthday, so we return to the theory that he added two years for each birthday.

But, here is the pay-off! At the time of Spalding's death, his wallet contained two driver's licenses, one for the state of California and one for New Mexico. It is to be remembered that the information given on the application for a driver's license is sworn to be true and Spalding swore his correct birthdate was May 26, 1904! That date appears on both licenses. I submit, herewith, proof of my statement.

The story behind the story of his birthdate of May 26, 1904, is that authorities refused to grant him a license to drive because of his age. The next time Spalding applied for a license, he removed that stumbling block. His New Mexico license was restricted to an area within a few miles of his mining claims. He had little respect for restrictions of any kind and this one did not hamper him. He made many trips to Los Angeles driving on the restricted license and died in Arizona with it in his pocket.

I confirmed statements concerning his remarkable energy. For the present, we will assume he was really 95 years old. During his last year, he piloted an airplane over several of the western states. He did not own a plane but it was not uncommon for him to charter one. He was forbidden to carry passengers, another restriction which he ignored. I talked with a man who said Spalding flew him from Los Angeles to New Mexico in the summer of 1952.

The Fabulous Baird T. Spalding

He drove an automobile up to within twelve hours of his death. His cruising speed was 80 miles an hour if the car would go that fast; otherwise, as fast as it could go.

During the last two weeks he lived he traveled more than 4,000 miles by auto. I have a sales receipt for the purchase of gasoline in New Mexico on March 17, 1953. He registered in a motel in Tempe, Arizona before midnight of the same day. He had driven more than 400 miles from where the gasoline was bought and had made two or three business stops. This time, he was driving a half-ton truck, not a passenger car.

During his last year, he made several trips from New Mexico to Los Angeles driving this same truck. The distance is 859 miles. Spalding drove straight through without rest and after two or three hours of sleep he could drive the return trip. I am not sure whether he ever did this or not.

A month before Spalding died, he packed on his back a mining drill, weighing 60 pounds, over eight miles of rugged New Mexico terrain. When he arrived at his destination he used the drill for a week, drilling twenty-four consecutive hours on one occasion.

Spalding's fabulous mind did not seem to be inhibited

by thinking processes. Rather than thinking, it seemed to "unreel." Invariably, when asked if he knew a certain person, he gave a standard reply, "Why, I knew him well." Just one time was I able to ask Baird if he had met someone and he confessed he had not. The one in question was Brigham Young. Spalding did say, though, when he was a small boy his father took him to hear Brigham Young speak but he did not meet him.

One evening, Spalding was reminiscing about early California days. My father-in-law came to California in 1905 and, just for the fun of it, I asked Baird if he ever met him.

"What was his name?" questioned Spalding.

"Charlie Porter," I replied.

"Why sure, I knew Charlie well." He related many facts about my father-in-law. He said he was a friend of Luther Burbank, that he worked in and near Pasadena, et cetera; in fact, Spalding claimed he met him in Pasadena, which is logical.

He finished by saying, "But Charlie is dead now. Died in 1933, didn't he?"

The Fabulous Baird T. Spalding

I answered, "Yes, Baird. October third, to be exact." I wanted to inform him of just one little detail.

While still in this mood, Spalding spoke of being in the vicinity of Big Bear Lake (of Southern California) many years ago. I asked if he had ever known a person by the name of Bert Gay who drove a supply wagon from San Bernardino to Big Bear about that same time.

"I knew Bert well," came the familiar reply. He told me, among other things, the number of horses Gay drove, the cargo he hauled and how much pay he received per pound. I knew the story was true because Gay had already mentioned it to me. A few days later, I saw Bert Gay and asked him if he ever knew anyone by the name of Baird T. Spalding in those early days of Big Bear. He told me, emphatically, he did not even know the name of Baird T. Spalding.

Some people I knew had recently purchased an old gold mine in Northern California. I attempted to tell Spalding about the mine but could not recall its name or location.

Finally, I remembered one landmark. A prehistoric river had run along the base of the hill near the mine. Spalding took it from there and gave me a complete history of it. As he talked, my memory was activated and I recalled the story the new owners had told me. Two sisters had owned the mine for years. They sold it to the people I knew. Spalding mentioned them and said they were now living at a certain address.

"No," I interrupted. "Caroline died about three months ago."

"Well!" exclaimed Spalding. "I didn't know that."

It was not impossible to take him off guard but it was certainly difficult. If anything surprised him he said "Well!" — very quickly and with emphasis.

People have expressed the opinion to me that they thought Spalding read minds. The fact that I knew of the death of one of the two sisters and he was surprised by the news would indicate that he was not reading my mind.

He told the history of several Arizona mines which I later found to be true. He described the Old Thompson Castle, the furnishings, Mr. Thompson's illness and other things of interest which I verified on a visit to the spot some months later.

Baird Spalding spent the greater part of his time prospecting and trying to develop mining claims. As nearly as I could determine, in settling his estate, not a single one of these projects ever realized any money for him. This seems odd for he, apparently, knew everything. Logically, one would expect him to locate valuable ore in great quantities with no difficulty at all. His mind did inspire confidence in many people to lend financial assistance to his endeavors. So confident were they that any agreement, other than Spalding's word, would have been a sacrilege. Only a few did not feel this way in lending him money.

One evening, Spalding was present when a discussion arose concerning the size tins used in packing sardines. One person said it was a six ounce tin, another said it was a ten ounce tin. Spalding's opinion was solicited and he replied, "You're both wrong. Sardines are packed in a seven ounce tin." As absolute proof, a trip was made to the market to buy sardines. They were packed in a seven ounce tin.

Not infrequently he was asked such a question as this: "Is it true that grass is really greener in some sections of the world than others?"

And the answer would spontaneously come forth, "Yes, in Ireland, an area of New Zealand and one in Alaska have greener grass due to a certain prevailing atmospheric condition . . . " and he would technically explain why.

The manner in which Spalding talked of places, people and events made the whole world seem about the size of a golf ball. His clarity of memory obliterated time; however, if he forgot anything he kept right on talking and his perplexed listener was deluged by a strange mixture of fact and fiction. Sometimes, when conversation was a little dull, Spalding would whip in one which was startling enough to wake up the crowd. For instance, here is one he told.

When Spalding was in India, he was once crossing the Ganges in a small boat manned by natives. One of the crew put his hand over the side of the boat and an alligator bit it off at the wrist. When they reached the opposite side of the river, one of the Masters who was present to meet him took pity on the poor native and restored his lost hand.

This is a wonderful story which adequately illustrates the power and great compassion the Masters hold for humanity. It is truly a remarkable incident to witness. The only thing wrong with it is — there are no alligators in this area of the Ganges!

The India Tour of 1935 marked Baird T. Spalding's

first and only trip to that country. I have established this fact to my complete satisfaction. In doing research for this book, I have discussed the India Tour with three members of the party. Their reports agree on the experiences of this trip. I shall repeat only a few of them. They were filled with pathos, humor and disappointment and more space than I can allow is required to do them justice.

Doug DeVorss gave me my first version of Spalding's trip to India. It does not check with those who were on the tour. Doug gave Baird the starring role and left the impression with me that Spalding assisted other members of the party with their enlightenment while in India.

I was never able to ascertain exactly why the India Tour was made. I have had several reasons offered me which range from the benevolence of Spalding to the "chosen few" to the few people who felt sorry for Spalding and wanted him to visit India before he died. It would not surprise me if a mixture of these two extremes might furnish a fairly accurate reason for the trip. I can see where the "benevolent" Spalding might chance meeting someone outstanding and desire to accompany the group to India; on the other hand, I can understand a group, not sure whether or not Spalding had connections in India, wanting to see for themselves. In the latter case, if he had not been there, they would want him to go.

Baird T. Spalding As I Knew Him

According to my informants who made the India trip, Spalding had talked a great deal of his Rest Home located on the Ganges River above Calcutta. He made it sound so fascinating that a group decided to go there and visit it. Before they docked, Spalding warned them the roads were impassable to the Rest Home and the only way they could get there was by horseback. There were several couples in the crowd and, naturally, if the ladies did not feel they could endure the strain of horseback travel, it was unlikely the men would insist on going. This was a pretty safe alibi for Spalding not wanting to go to the Rest Home. However, the unexpected happened and the ladies thought that seeing the Rest Home would be worth the hardships of the trip. Spalding became very angry at this, accused some of them of distrusting his word and finally said the Rest Home had been totally destroyed by an earthquake which plunged it into the river.

He also promised that at least one Master would meet them at the boat when they arrived. It is needless to say, this did not happen.

Spalding deserted the India party on arrival. No one of the group saw him again until almost time to come back to America. By this time, Spalding was out of funds and had no return ticket. A member of the party bought first class passage for him and gave him the ticket. He turned the ticket in for cash and came back to America on a freighter. He went to India with a party of friends but came home alone.

I think the foregoing incidents are sufficient to establish my point that some people, at least, had grounds for believing that Spalding was not as careful with the truth as he might have been.

The following stories I relate as they were told to me. I have absolutely no verification of them; however, they originated with highly reputable persons. I found them to be very interesting because they illustrate so well the type of thing accredited to Spalding.

When Hoover Dam was built, the chief problem was in cooling the cement. It was estimated the process would take approximately one hundred years. The engineers were unable to find a short-cut. As a last resort, someone suggested calling in Baird T. Spalding. According to my informant, Spalding suggested circulating ice water through the structure and let the pipes serve a dual purpose, that of cooling and giving additional strength. This was the method used in cooling Hoover Dam and the time element was cut to three and a half years.

Spalding once remarked to a gentleman that he and his father built the first railroad in Japan. This was an insult to the man's intelligence. Months later, this man's son was stationed in the armed forces in Japan. He wrote his son and asked him to find out who built the first railroad there. The son took some time investigating this matter and then wrote his father that it was built by a man named Spalding. The railroad still bears his name.

It is my understanding that Baird T. Spalding never filed an income tax. It was reliably reported to me that the Department of Internal Revenue spent several weeks looking into this matter in the state of California about three years ago. They were unable to locate a legitimate reason why he should pay income tax and discontinued their investigation. About a year before Spalding's death, the Internal Revenue Agents again became interested in his income. This time it was in New Mexico. After two agents spent three weeks checking Spalding they told a member of the legal profession, "We have never seen anyone live so well on nothing."

The idea that Spalding lacked money will naturally raise many questions in the minds of those who read this. It does in mine, too. I have a tape recording wherein Douglas K. DeVorss makes a public statement that Spalding's books had sold over a million copies in the English language alone. Royalties from this amount of book sales should amount to a comfortable sum of money. However,

Spalding claimed that DeVorss did not pay him any royalties for a period of thirteen years; further, that he never received anything for the Fourth Volume. I have no way of verifying these statements. Doug once told me he arranged for the Fourth Volume talks to be taken in shorthand and sent to him. The publication of this Volume was to have repaid DeVorss $2,000 which he said he advanced Spalding so he could make the trip to India. I have talked with another person who declared he financed Spalding's trip and that DeVorss did not lend him the money so here we go again. I am sure Spalding did not reap any monetary gain from the Fourth Volume.

I do know DeVorss had a contract with Spalding which paid Spalding a stipulated sum for life. DeVorss intimated to me this amount was five hundred dollars per month but more recent information states it was only one hundred and fifty dollars. The Spalding books have brought a handsome profit to the publisher; in fact, so much that DeVorss entertained a guilt complex about it. Shortly after Spalding died, DeVorss told me he was setting up a non-profit corporation to perpetuate the Spalding books. I did not believe this but it would be to DeVorss' advantage for me, as Administrator of the Spalding estate, to pass such news around. About three months later, DeVorss told me the incorporation papers had been approved and there was now a definite Spalding Foundation. The Executor of

DeVorss' estate never located any such papers.

For some reason, when Spalding wrote DeVorss, his letters always began: "Dear Dug:" I am sure he knew how to spell the abbreviation for "Douglas."

Many people have asked me if Mr. Spalding were ever married. He was married but had no children. Mrs. Spalding died several years ago.

Just one occurrence came to my attention, which I considered authentic, in regard to Spalding having any knowledge of occult power. Some friends told me he visited them one evening and they asked him if he was familiar with a certain book which was filled with technical data. He said he was not but asked to see a copy of it. He placed the book over his heart and talked, as usual, for two hours or more. He did not take the book home with him. The next morning he called at the house again and this time he was ready to discuss all phases of the book. This may, or may not, be an example of his occult knowledge.

One lady told me that when Spalding was in South America she kept a daily record of her astral projections to him. On his return she showed him the data and he said it was one hundred per cent correct. Personally, I do not think he was ever in South America; consequently, I could place no value on her report. It is self-evident how he could confirm her findings, though.

Spalding maintained that "Emil" lived on his ranch in South America. He promised to bring him to Los Angeles in January, 1953. Many of his friends and acquaintances were looking forward to the opportunity of meeting Emil. I do not recall why Emil's trip did not materialize but this tale is in the same category with his "Rest Home" in India.

Doug DeVorss, in setting up Spalding to be a highly spiritual type of man, often referred to Spalding as "eating like a bird." While I have heard Spalding say that if one is seeking enlightenment he should not eat meat, that did not stop him from eating it. For those who may be interested, I publish Baird T. Spalding's standard breakfast menu as of two weeks prior to his death.

> Fruit
> Hot cereal
> Buckwheat cakes
> Ham and eggs with fried potatoes
> Toast
> Coffee

Baird was not adverse to consulting doctors in regard to his health. I might add, too, that he seldom carried out their advice but he would take medicine for a short period of time. He was hospitalized for several days a few months before he died.

Baird T. Spalding As I Knew Him

I found Baird Spalding to have a keen appreciation for the arts and beauty. He was especially fond of poetry. He seldom quoted another writer in any of his talks but one night, in a private gathering, he quoted Shakespeare at length.

Flowers and natural scenes were his idea of true beauty. He often remarked that the perfection found in flowers was a continuation of universal perfection. He said if one looked for perfection he could find it in all things.

Spalding was a very kind person. He was kind to every living thing. His most outstanding trait was gentleness. These qualities, plus his good disposition, endeared him to many people.

Just before he died, he was walking down the street in a small New Mexico town and met a lady whom he knew only by sight. Her home had recently undergone disaster. Spalding handed her over four hundred dollars in cash saying, "This might come in handy." He never saw her again.

Some people have told me Spalding was nothing but a confidence man and that he spent his time trying to cheat his friends out of enough money to become rich. Definitely, I do not believe this. With the reverence shown to

THE FABULOUS BAIRD T. SPALDING

Baird T. Spalding,, he could have easily promoted one of the most colossal religious rackets of modern times. This would have coined him money by the millions. Too much credit cannot be given Spalding for his lack of interest in commercializing and exploiting religion for money and personal aggrandizement. He had no organization, whatsoever.

Because the pendulum of Spalding's personality swung across such a wide arc which contained contradictions, falsities, deception, kindness, gentleness, selfishness, generosity, anger, hatred and love for his fellowman (as well as combinations of these), it is very difficult to present a comprehensive picture of him. The shortest, and probably the most effective, description of him is that he was fantastic — and fabulous.

73

SPALDING'S DEATH

CHAPTER FIVE

I spoke in Scottsdale, Arizona on Sunday evening, March 15, 1953. As is my custom, my talk was followed by a "Questions and Answers" period. A lady addressed me:

"Do you know Baird T. Spalding?"

Answer: "Yes, I know Mr. Spalding very well."

Question: "Is he a Master?"

Answer: "Definitely not."

Question: "How old is he?"

Answer: "Mr. Spalding says he is 95 years old."

Question: "How old does he look?"

Answer: "Ninety-five."

Had I taken less than a realistic view of Baird Spalding I would have suffered no little embarrassment at the announcement of his death three days later.

BAIRD T. SPALDING *As I Knew Him*

I returned to my temporary headquarters in Hollywood from our home in Phoenix on Tuesday, March 17. On the morning of March 18 I arose early and continued some writings that were in progress when I left for Arizona. Spalding was not on my mind and I had not thought of him since the previous Sunday evening. My attention was thoroughly trained on what I was doing when a voice, almost like someone speaking over a telephone, said, "Baird Spalding is dead — or will be in a few minutes." This was between ten and eleven o'clock, Pacific Standard Time, Wednesday morning. On Arizona time, this was between eleven and twelve o'clock. I thought this a very strange experience for I instinctively knew the information was true. Several times in the next few hours I thought of the experience but I was very busy and did not stop to analyze it. I was still working about three o'clock in the afternoon when the voice said again, "Baird Spalding is dead."

Let me state, definitely and plainly, that I am not one who "hears voices." This occurs with me only under the rarest circumstances. When I am clairaudient, it is under my direction. I wish to make it clear that I do not encourage, for myself or others, the development of psychic powers or extra-sensory perception.

Spalding registered at a Tempe motel about 11:30 Tuesday night. Apparently, he was exhausted because, in

76

signing the register, his hand shook so badly that his signature was almost illegible. He did not give a home address on the registration card.

About ten o'clock Wednesday morning, one of the guests in an adjoining cabin saw Spalding go to his truck and, after a few minutes, return to his quarters. Checkout time for the motel was 10:00 A.M. When guests arrived late at night, the owner usually permitted them to stay until noon before starting another day. Between 11:30 and 12:00 noon, the owner called at Spalding's door to ask if he wanted to stay another day. The door was slightly ajar. When his knock met with no response, the owner entered Spalding's room. The upper part of Spalding's body was sprawled across the bed with his feet on the floor. He had evidently failed in his attempt to reach the bed.

This room was heated with an open flame gas burner which caused the owner to think his guest had succumbed to asphyxiation. He called the fire department who rushed their resuscitation equipment which they used without effect. It was later determined that the gas heater was not involved in Spalding's death.

Baird T. Spalding, known to millions of people throughout the world, took the final initiation of this life alone. He was the third world figure in recent years to make his exit without the presence of doctors or friends. King George slipped away in his sleep and Henry Ford passed on with no one but Mrs. Ford there.

Establishing Spalding's identification was a little difficult. His driver's license used the name of "Baird Thomas Spalding" but the age on the license did not match that of the man in question. Other papers in Spalding's possession bore the name of "Baird T. Grey," a name he often used to escape his public. There were no marks of identification with the "Grey" papers. To complicate matters, one piece of luggage was initialed, "T. L. S." The truck had New Mexico license plates and his driver's license for that state gave a New Mexico address. His California driver's license gave a California address and both licenses were active. The Tempe Daily News, on March 18th, ran a short article on Spalding's death. It was captioned: "Authorities Check on Death at Court."

Late Wednesday afternoon, news of Spalding's death reached Mrs. Ruth Welsch in whose home Spalding kept a room. Mrs. Welsch was unable to contact DeVorss until Thursday morning.

DeVorss had no sooner been informed of Spalding's death than he called me to see if I could go to Arizona and take charge of his funeral services. Due to commitments here, it seemed impossible for me to take the time for a return trip to Arizona at the moment. I told DeVorss I would call him back within the hour and give him my answer.

In the meantime, I called Ida Hagan Marshall who had known Spalding for many years. I told her of Baird's death and that I had been called to take charge of his funeral. She urged me to go saying, "By all means go, David. You can say something that will help send the old fellow on his way." Despite my accumulated work I felt I should honor DeVorss' request. I called Doug and said I would go if the funeral services could be held the following Sunday afternoon. I would leave Friday evening.

Under the circumstances, I was not at all flattered by DeVorss asking me to conduct the Spalding rites. It always made Doug nervous for me to mention Spalding for he was aware that I knew a great deal of Baird's history as well as his lack of experiences in India. Because I was not taken in by the Spalding myth, Doug felt there was a chance I might make some statements about it. He knew I was fond of Baird and, undoubtedly, gambled that my personal feeling would carry me through a credible memorial talk. Doug was an opportunist and he knew my name would look well on this occasion for it had often been associated with Spalding. Then, too, there was a little matter of money. DeVorss was determined to get through the last expenses of Spalding as cheaply as possible. He knew I would request no fee for my services and that if he asked anyone else qualified to conduct this service, the charge would be more than he cared to pay. In other words, I was conscious of the fact DeVorss thought he was taking advantage of me at this time rather than paying me a compliment.

The question of what to do with Spalding's remains was discussed. DeVorss first wanted the body shipped back to California and a second funeral held as requested by many of Spalding's old friends. After the California service, DeVorss wanted to bury his body.

On more than one occasion I had talked about death with Baird Spalding. He had no respect whatsoever for a dead body. He thought cremation to be the only "sanitary and sensible" thing to do after death and he told me the ashes should be scattered. His exact words when I asked him what he thought should be done with physical remains were, "What difference does it make?" Then, he spoke of the logical thing to do. I could not see any reason to discard Spalding's wishes so I insisted that his body be cremated and his ashes scattered in Arizona. Doug gave me a letter stating my authority to do as I wished.

Spalding's Death

About an hour before I was to leave, DeVorss telephoned and asked if he could go along. This was agreeable with me and, I might add, in line with my anticipations. Irvin Palmer, my personal manager, Douglas K. DeVorss and I left for Arizona on Friday evening, March 20, to pay our last respects to Baird T. Spalding.

Shortly after our arrival in Phoenix the following morning we went to the Carr Mortuary for the purpose of identifying Spalding's body and making the funeral arrangements. Next, we went to the Coroner's office to inquire what steps were to be taken for the release of Spalding's effects. Doug flashed a photostat copy of a holographic Will made by Spalding wherein he gave Douglas K. DeVorss his books at his death. No provision was made by Spalding for disposing of any other property, real or personal, in this Will or any other Will; therefore, DeVorss became sole heir of the Spalding estate.

The Coroner advised DeVorss that an administrator for the estate of Baird T. Spalding would have to be appointed by the Superior Court of Arizona and that the appointee was required to be a resident of Arizona.

"Why can't Mr. Bruton be appointed administrator? He is a resident of Arizona," asked Doug.

Baird T. Spalding *As I Knew Him*

I had maintained a residence in Arizona since 1950, a matter that was easy to verify.

It was agreed that I was qualified to serve as Spalding's administrator and I would receive my appointment to this effect on Monday.

None of us knew how many people to expect for Spalding's Memorial Service. News of his death was so late getting to the Los Angeles papers that only a small item appeared. One long article appeared in the Phoenix paper but it was captioned: "L.A. Author, 97, Dies in Tempe Auto Court." We decided to hold the service in the Carr Mortuary Chapel which seated approximately one hundred. We had plenty of room for it was about three-fourths full. Several people drove from Los Angeles for the service. One lady who went on the India Tour with Spalding was wintering in Phoenix and attended.

I wanted to make one point in my talk in behalf of Baird T. Spalding for it conveyed my honest conviction about him. Whether or not he experienced the things he wrote about is unimportant. The fact that he presented the Masters as living Beings and placed the attainment of Mastership within the grasp of each individual was the important destiny Spalding fulfilled. He made the Masters real to the multitudes without lowering the status of the

Master. He raised the single consciousness to a point of realization of his own Mastership, no matter how fleeting the experience may have been. No other group, or person, has been able to put across such a realistic approach coupled with a widespread appeal as did Spalding. I mentioned that the publication of his Volume One marked a new era in spiritual unfoldment just as definitely as did the dropping of the atom bomb usher us into the atomic age. My talk was sincere for, while I saw the flaws in Spalding's personality, I also admitted his valuable contribution to world enlightenment.

Here are my closing words:

"I do not prefer a conventional benediction for our friend, Baird Spalding. I feel it would not become him. One of his favorite topics of conversation was the Light that lighteth every man. So, let us know:

"There is a Light that lighteth every man that cometh into the world. That Light is eternal, It is All-Powerful and It is imperishable. 'Only that which is subject to birth is subject to death'; the Light is not born and, therefore, cannot die. It is a creation of God, an unsegmented segment of the Whole.

"Let us wish Baird Spalding God speed in his greater expansion."

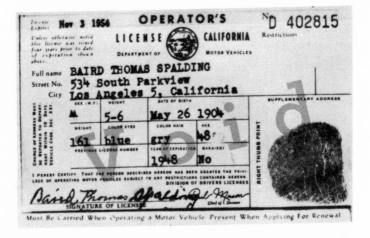

California operator's license showing the date of
Baird T. Spalding's birth as May 26, 1904.

CERTIFICATE OF CREMATION

Greenwood Memorial Park Crematory

Phoenix, Arizona, _____March 24_____, 19 53

THIS IS TO CERTIFY:

That _____Baird Thomas Spalding_____

HAS BEEN CREMATED AT GREENWOOD MEMORIAL PARK CREMATORY,

UNDER OBSERVANCE OF ALL LEGAL REQUIREMENTS, on the

_____23rd_____ **Day of** _____March_____ 19 53

Sex _____Male_____ Color _____Cauc_____ Age _____95_____

Usual Address _____Los Angeles, California_____

Place of Death _____Tmpe, Arizona_____

Date of Death _____March 18, 1953_____

Cause of Death _____Apparently cardiac failure_____

Medical Attendant _____Ralph W. Fowler, Coroner_____

Mortician _____Carr Mortuary_____

Register No. _____27506_____

GREENWOOD MEMORIAL PARK CREMATORY

By _____S.R. Newton_____
Superintendent.

Certificate of cremation for Baird Thomas Spalding.

IN THE SUPERIOR COURT
OF MARICOPA COUNTY, STATE OF ARIZONA

31022

IN THE MATTER OF THE ESTATE

of

Baird T. Spalding

Deceased.

No.................

ORDER
APPOINTING ADMINISTRATOR

The affidavit of........David Bruton.., having been duly filed

and presented in Court, and the Court having considered the same, and being satisfied that the said

............Baird T. Spalding..is deceased, and in need of some

fit and proper person to act as Administrator of the estate; that the entire estate of said deceased within

the state of Arizona, is less than $500.00.

And it appearing that the said......David Bruton...................is a fit and proper person to

act as such Administrator of the estate of..................Baird T. Spalding................................

IT IS THEREFORE ORDERED, ADJUDGED AND DECREED that the said....David Bruton...........

....be, and hereby is, appointed Administrator of the estate of said deceased,

......Baird T. Spalding...within the provisions of Section 38, 1901

Arizona Code Annotated, 1939, as amended.

Done in open Court, this.......23.................day of........March................................, 193......

FRANCIS J. DONOFRIO

Endorsed No ____ **31022**

Filed: WALTER S. WILSON, Clerk

at 4:25 PM

By Hazel Cardwell, Deputy

March 23, 1953

Judge.

STATE OF ARIZONA }
County of Maricopa } ss.

I, WALTER S. WILSON, Clerk of the Superior Court of Maricopa County, State of Arizona, hereby

certify that I have compared the foregoing copy with the original Order Appointing Administrator in the

above entitled matter filed in my office on the...23.........day of......March..................., A.D. 195.3.,

and that the same is a true copy of the original and of the whole thereof.

Witness my hand and the seal of said Court, this.....23.........................day of

..................................March.., A.D. 195.3.

WALTER S. WILSON
Clerk

By ....
Deputy Clerk.

Order appointing administrator of the estate of
Baird T. Spalding.

**IN THE SUPERIOR COURT OF THE STATE OF ARIZONA
IN AND FOR THE COUNTY OF MARICOPA**

IN THE MATTER OF THE ESTATE

of

........Baird T. Spalding........

Deceased.

No. **31022**

DECREE OF DISTRIBUTION

It appearing to the Court that the value of the estate of the deceased is less than $500.00, it is now ORDERED and DECREED that the whole of said estate, consisting of the following described personal property, to-wit:

......1947 International KB2 Motor No. GRD 214-177451 Serial No. 45396......

......Cash in the amount of $15.98 Watch and other personal belongings......

be and the same is hereby set aside and distributed to......Douglas K. DeVorss......

DONE IN OPEN COURT this the......23......day of......March......, 195..3..

Endorsed No. **31022**

Filed: WALTER S. WILSON, Clerk
at 4:25 PM
By Hazel Cardwell, Deputy
March 23, 1953

FRANCIS J. DONOFRIO

Judge

Decree of Distribution of the Baird T. Spalding estate.

David Bruton in Papago Park, Arizona, holding the box containing the ashes of Baird T. Spalding, just before scattering them.

David Bruton scattering the ashes of Baird T. Spalding in Papago Park, near Phoenix, Arizona.

The last known picture of Baird Thomas Spalding, courtesy
of Rev. S. S. Heyliager, Hollywood, Calif.

BAIRD T. SPALDING AFTER DEATH

Chapter Six

Due to my occult training, I am emphatically opposed to "contacting " or otherwise disturbing the so-called dead. After one withdraws from his body on this plane he is magnetically relocated, through karma, into another realm of activity. Whatever his new status may be and whatever experience awaits him there is for his learning just as his physical life contributed to that same learning. It is not fair to the one who has gone ahead for those who remain here to selfishly pull him back into a phase of life which he has temporarily finished. We should not attempt to bind him to our own physical desire in a plane where he cannot legitimately operate.

Each individual should realize that he is not dependent on another, living or dead, for the personal knowledge of how to direct his own affairs. Physical problems can best be solved on the physical plane by parties whose interest is centered here. Those who have discarded their physical bodies soon lose the perspective of life as we know it and are not as well qualified to lend physical aid as are the ones who still live in the flesh. Everyone draws his knowledge from the Universal Mind but the plane from whence he contacts It determines his viewpoint.

Without resorting to mediumship, or giving up one's body for the purpose of obsession by a discarnate soul, as each individual progresses in his learning his consciousness expands, naturally, to include sensitivity of other planes than the physical. When this development takes place it is possible to converse with the "dead" in precisely the same manner that we talk with the living. When one reaches that degree of evolvement he is no longer curious of conditions after death and will not interfere with the processing of Life as it is guided by Those who watch the over-all picture. I make these statements to clearly define my personal stand because of the incidents which follow.

On the evening of April 11, 1953, I was included in a group who attended a demonstration of telekenesis, or "table knocking," as it is sometimes called. This experience was distinctly against my wishes but my host and hostess were unyielding in the insistance that I should witness such a demonstration. I submit the following as an accurate transcript of my one and only telekenesis experience.

Two ladies sat opposite each other and placed their hands, palms down, on an ordinary card table. The room was dark. Immediately, the table began to respond. The operators were in contact with the medium's late son, Rex, who was killed in battle during World War II. The technique of communication was explained in this manner:

The side of the table where the medium sat lifted and dropped to the floor. The sound was considered a "knock." One knock meant "no," two knocks, "uncertain, maybe, could be," three knocks, "yes." Loud knocks were used for emphasis, "skipping" knocks for playfulness and the table actually "waved" for laughter. Short, quick thumps on the floor was the method used for spelling. One thump "a," two thumps, "b," three thumps, "c," et cetera.

Shortly after greetings were exchanged between Rex and the medium and we, the guests, were properly welcomed, the card table began moving toward me. It was very insistent.

The lady seated with the medium asked, "Does someone want to talk to David?"

Three knocks replied, "Yes."

"Is it a man or a woman?" someone asked Rex.

No answer.

"Is it a woman?"

One knock, "No."

"Give me the initial of the man's name," I requested.

Two short thumps, "B."

"Baird Spalding?" I asked.

Three knocks which were almost wild, "Yes!"

"Is there something Mr. Spalding wants to say?" I asked.

Three knocks, "Yes."

"Am I talking to Baird Spalding?" was my next question.

Three knocks, "Yes."

Someone asked, "Can Mr. Spalding operate the table?"

One knock, "No."

Then it was explained by the medium that Mr. Spald-

94

ing had not been on the other side long enough to learn how to operate the table. This, it seems, is quite a feat. Our communication would be transmitted through Rex, such as one might speak to another through an interpreter.

I asked, "Is there another Will besides the one we already have?"

One knock, "No."

"Is there anything in particular I should know about your estate?"

One knock, "No."

I asked a few personal questions in regard to the estate and, then:

"Did Mr. Spalding know he was going to die?"

Three strong knocks, "Yes."

"A long while before he died?"

Three solid knocks, "Yes."

"Was your correct age 95?"

Three knocks, "Yes."

"Did Baird approve of my disposition of his ashes?"

Three emphatic knocks, "Yes."

"Did he approve of my talk at his funeral?"

Again three emphatic knocks, "Yes."

"Wasn't Baird Spalding one of the most important persons to have lived during the past few hundred years?"

Very strong, three knocks, "Yes."

"Should I write the book on Baird's life?"

Three violent knocks, "YES."

"Am I better qualified to write on his life than anyone else?"

Three very heavy knocks, "Yes."

"A humorous slant to the book alright?"

Three knocks, "Yes."

"Is there any particular angle Baird wants mentioned in the book?"

Then came spelling, "L-o-v-e f-o-r h-u-m-a-n-i-t-y."

You want it stressed that you had a great love for humanity?" I asked.

Three knocks, "Yes."

"What, from the other side, is the most important thing you learned in life here?"

Again, spelling: "T-o-l-e-r-a-n-c-e."

"I shall stress your love for humanity and tolerance for all people if they are to gain world peace?"

Three loud knocks, "Yes."

"Should DeVorss publish the book?"

"Two indifferent knocks, "Maybe."

"Someone else?"

Two more indifferent knocks, "Maybe."

"Do you want to tell me anything else?" was my final question.

The rapid tappings of spelling began:

"G-o-d B-l-e-s-s Y-o-u."

Baird Thomas Spalding had again faded from the senses of the world.

The medium asked Rex, "Were there many people waiting to meet Mr. Spalding when he arrived on the other side?"

Three loud knocks, "Yes."

"Great crowds?" she continued.

Three more loud knocks, "Yes."

Irvin Palmer asked, "Is Spalding still there?"

One knock, "No."

I explained it was very difficult for Spalding to focus his attention enough to make and hold this contact.

The table confirmed my statement by knocking three times.

Baird T. Spalding After Death

Irving asked another question, "Does Spalding get around as much over there as he did here?"

Three gay little taps came from the table and then it began to wave.

I asked if Rex sought Mr. Spalding on the other side.

One knock, "No."

Rex explained they were attracted into the same unit because of mutual interests in religion, philosophy and humanity.

Thus ended the telekenetic contact with Baird T. Spalding.

* * * *

On Sunday evening, April 12, 1953, I retired shortly before midnight. I was not at all sleepy. I tossed restlessly for some minutes and suddenly, a phonetic impression came, saying, "Baird Spalding is here."

I sat up in bed and saw Baird standing in the room. After a cordial, "Hello, there," we began talking just the same as we had always done.

Baird T. Spalding As I Knew Him

Mr. Spalding was dressed in a dark blue suit, white shirt and a dark tie. He looked many years younger than he did when I last saw him. His general appearance was that of a person who had just returned from a refreshing vacation, full of vitality and health.

Of course, this was not the first time I had conversed with one who had passed through the portal of death. I learned a long while ago that we who remain on this physical plane put the stamp of finality on death. The ones who have passed to the other side of the curtain are as much alive as they ever were and they know it. Not being able to see and converse with the "departed" is due to the fact that we completely shut them out. The mass of humanity is hypnotised by the fear of death and superstitions of heaven and hell. Perhaps seventy-five or more of the so-called "dead" have appeared to me and talked with me during the past twenty years. If one is welcome to come to me on this side of Life, I do not exclude him if he moves to another plane. It should be understood, I never seek anyone after they experience death any more than I would seek them before death. If anyone appears to me more than once I talk to him about his own progress and that he should give his attention to his new opportunity for learning.

My conversation with Baird was more or less a confirmation of the telekenesis contact on the previous evening. I asked additional questions in regard to his estate and, again, if there was another Will. He told me he had intended to make a new Will very soon but "I didn't get around to it" as he put it. When I asked him again if he had known of his impending death he said he did. He had known it for some time. He said he had suffered a cardiac condition and knew he could not last much longer. During our discussion of his death, Spalding made the statement: "I expected to live two weeks longer than I did." Several days later I checked this date on the calendar. It was April First!

Baird held this contact with me as long as he possibly could. His answers became indefinite and incoherent as he gradually faded away. Spalding was gone again. He never attempted to return to me so far as I know.

While the appearance of Baird Spalding was not, in itself, unusual to me, however, this is the first time I ever conducted one's funeral, ordered the body cremated and scattered his ashes and then had him return to me for a nice friendly chat. If I had still entertained any doubts of the continuity of Life, this experience would have dispelled them. I have often thought that my final parting with Baird was a proper climax to my unique association with him.

CONCLUSION

Because of my relatively short acquaintance with **Baird T. Spalding**, several people have intimated that I should not have undertaken the task of writing his life story. If knowing is to be gauged in time, then I can agree that three years is not long enough to gather a picture of anyone's life. If time is not the only factor involved in knowing, or, if knowing takes place in a timeless realm, that of mind, then it must be admitted that a fleeting second may hold a wealth of knowledge.

Ways and means of looking into one's life are known that enables one possessing such knowledge to hastily bridge the years. If one is now the sum total of his past, there must be something in the present which displays a composite of all preceding time; for instance, the aura contains much of this information. Gestures, mannerisms, traits of mind, habits of speech, physical appearance, importance and unimportance of events, the individual's viewpoint on life and hosts of other mental and physical characteristics supply keys that quickly open tiny doors into the Akashic Records. In view of these facts, time shrinks in importance.

A grand picture may sweep before one's eyes as he

meets another. No matter how long he knows him, all acts in the future will merely confirm the original picture. I do not hesitate to express my views on Spalding because I knew him but a short time. In his own words, I may say that "I knew him well!"

Information concerning Baird T. Spalding has found its way to me in an incredible manner. It has come from the most authentic sources; even so, I have found it necessary to discount a liberal percentage of it. Those who are in a position to give extensive insight into his life are, as a rule, biased in their opinions. I have observed repeatedly that if one had an unpleasant experience with Spalding, he disqualified the rest of Spalding's life. Usually, the unhappy contacts with him were due to money, loans, investments in Spalding ideas, mining ventures and the like. This side of Spalding was wholly unimportant when compared to his contribution toward world enlightenment. His money-making schemes were a recreation and pastime to him and, I believe, he thought there was always a possibility that something might come from one of them.

No one with whom I have talked seems to catch the idea that Spalding fulfilled an important destiny *regardless of anything else*. So far as the effect he produced is concerned, the origin of his manuscripts is unimportant, whether he was strictly truthful or, as one person remarked, "had no appreciation of the truth" is still unimportant. The books which bear his name as "author" cannot be minimized in the revolutionary changes they have fomented in the minds of his readers. I do not make this statement in defense of Spalding nor is it to be construed that I am condoning his personal life. Rather, I am attempting to appraise his work, as I see it, in connection with our times.

After no little deliberation, I decided to add this *"Conclusion."* It is my hope to give a fair and accurate picture of Spalding without destroying him. Those who have discovered a new Way of Life through his books naturally wish to cherish his memory. It is not my intention to rob them of this pleasure. My knowledge of him as a fellow human does not detract from the friendliness I felt toward him nor does it interfere with my acknowledging his worth as a conveyor of a message.

This statement was flung at me, "Why do you bother to write about Baird Spalding? He wasn't worth it."

When one passes from this phase of Life leaving behind him a trail of mystery and unresolved experiences, it impedes his progress on the other side. If we who remain here can, in any way, assist in finishing business he has left undone, we should do so. There is no reason why we should devote our life to such a cause but, if convenient, we can at least lend a helping hand in passing. We on the physical plane can often terminate points of contact for those whom we call the deceased and thereby lend our energies to the wheel of evolution as it turns. My responsibility in this writing, then, makes itself very clear if I am to help Baird Spalding at all. I am honor bound to present as true a picture of him as possible. I am aware that most of his reading public has been engulfed in the illusion about his life. This is due to the previous lack of factual information about him. This book may serve a dual purpose, that of release for Baird Spalding and to stabilize the thinking of those who followed his personality rather than the Principle of which he spoke. Mastership is a state of individual realization; therefore not transferrable to another. It is claimed only through the exercise of Principle, the Principle which summons to our consciousness the Truth of our Divinity. Each individual is endowed with an equal potential for attaining Mastership and is, therefore, accountable only to himself for the progress he makes, or fails to make, along the Path.

Spalding, the man who drew adoration from all over the world was really an object for pity. Frequently, he gave the impression that he was preoccupied because of a dreamy, far-away look in his eyes. At times, he had a vacant look as though he had almost abandoned his body. No one really understood him or could offer him suitable

companionship; consequently, he derived his greatest con-
tentment from roaming the wide open spaces alone. He
lived the last year of his life in an old shack with no modern
conveniences.

A highly reputable gentleman who professes clairvoyant
vision, and who had known Spalding for many years, told
me in an interview that Baird was under the control of
three astral entities. He said that Baird did not know
when he was speaking with a control and when he was
talking without one. He named the three controls as Baird's
grandfather, John Spalding, an old miner and a little child.

For those who are unacquainted with "astral controls"
it may be stated, briefly, that an astral control is a discarnate
being who, through his desire for expression on the earth-
plane, seizes any opportunity at hand whereby he can
obtain physical outlet for his desire. One living here who
exercises his desires (greed, hatred, jealousy, envy, egotism,
selfishness, et cetera) builds a bridge of contact into the
astral plane which permits the discarnate beings wishing to
express corresponding desires the use of a physical vehicle
necessary for an earth-plane expression. When an astral
entity has made the initial contact with one living here
it is comparatively easy for him to maintain and strengthen
the tie. Since all desire is rooted in fear our earth-plane
has become virtually a playground for astral exhibitions.

CONCLUSION

For example, greed, the fear of physical lack or inadequacy, encourages, or even invites, one who has passed through death with an unquenched thirst for the selfish acquirement of earthly possessions to join his greediness with one living physically; thus, through their mutual interests, a great mundane accomplishment may be effected. As a result, both the physical and non-physical entity, each of whom should be seeking the expression of his Universal Self in his respective sphere, become bound to each other in a state of insatiable desire. Usually, there is no release for either of them but a gradual exhaustion of energies.

Modern Christianity does not emphasize the pernicious effects of desire; in fact, a sprinkling of greed is often considered an asset in the business world and is not particularly frowned upon by the church. The Christian religion teaches, in short, that the experiences of Life are a springboard from which one jumps into the eternity of either heaven or hell and it is long overdue for expansion. Jesus taught that Life is a continuous action, or, as He stated, a "sowing and reaping."

Astral influences on our earth-plane are often referred to as activity of the Dark Forces. It is true that one who is polarized to the plane of desire is bereft of Light or a type of Self Expression which conforms to his purpose. Actually, the Dark Forces can operate through anyone, living or dead, if his interests are centered in the plane of desire. This situation, as it exists today, is perhaps the most serious of all problems facing humanity because the vast majority of human beings respond in some degree to the Dark Forces' influence. They thrive in confusion, fear and violence.

When an astral entity gains sufficient freedom in making contact with a physical means of gratifying his desires, either by frequent contact or intensity of desire on the part of one living here, the entity can gradually absorb the thinking processes of the individual to a degree that he can control his thoughts. Through desire, the living person surrenders his Self Expression to the god of desire. In Spalding's case, a definite influence of this nature was present. In other words, his life was not his own. Whether or not he was controlled by three astral entities is something I would hesitate to say. However, the clairvoyant with whom I talked was very definite in his assertions. I leave the decision, in this regard, to each of you.

My informant stated that when Spalding's thoughts were directed to India he instantly attracted his control, John Spalding, to supply him with information. Baird then spoke fluently about Hindu customs, their religious teachings and various phases of Indian life. His knowledge was automatic and required no thinking on Baird's part. Much of it was as new to him when he said it as it was to those who heard him because he did not know it, either.

As an explanation of Spalding's mind, it is logical to think there may have been a second control present, too. The "old miner" instinct surpassed all of the rest of Spalding's desires. To a casual observer, it seems that to endure the hardships encountered in prospecting one would need a deep desire. Is it not in line with good reasoning to suppose that countless miners who never struck it rich would, after death, happily release their unrequitted passion into another body to carry on their quest? Again, when Spalding's attention was turned to mining he came up with the right answers and his opinions were generally regarded as sound. On his own mining claims he dreamed of fabulous wealth to be taken from the earth.

In a placid or inactive mood, Baird T. Spalding was like a child. Most of his friends attributed his childishness to old age but I observed him carefully and it seemed a little different than that kind of childishness. Often, he seemed to have the mind of a child and he thought like a child. He played little games in his mind that gave an air of importance to whatever he was doing. Sometimes, the key to his thoughts was secluded in a play on words. He loved to tell the truth in a veiled way. For example, he set April Fool's Day for a day of change in all of his business affairs. He expected to die that day and there were no big deals being closed then, anyway. On the premise of his child-like qualities, I have strongly suspected that the "Spalding Foundation" in "India" is really a pile of rocks located in a remote desert region where he buried money. According to him, he put all of his money in the "Spalding Foundation." If he used the occult meaning of the word "India" (hidden), he could tell the truth to all who asked him for contributions and still not give them anything. When he went to "India" it amounted to no more than another mining venture in one of the western states.

Doug DeVorss was completely baffled by Spalding and made no pretense of explaining him. Doug was aware of the vast range of information which coursed through Spalding's head and he knew, too, that Spalding was said to have been under the control of three astral entities. When we were discussing Spalding, Doug frequently remarked, "You know, Baird has a 'thriple' personality," as he put it.

I knew, the first day I met Spalding, that he was a victim of astral obsession. I think the obsession, or obsessions, satisfactorily account for his ability to answer questions so readily. Perhaps, they also lend reason for the extreme opposites he displayed in his personality. Under most circumstances, I think Spalding sincerely believed what he said to be the truth. If there were exceptions, it was probably due to his speaking without a control. A photographic mind, working in conjunction with astral controls, would certainly offer a phenomenal scope of combinations.

I knew, also, on the day of our first visit with Spalding that he had not been to India prior to 1935 and that he had not experienced any of the recorded happenings in his books. If he were unwilling to safeguard the great illusions surrounding his books and would openly admit to me they were not true, then why should I be concerned about the Spalding myth becoming known? His admission to me came about in this manner:

We were discussing the Spalding "Time Camera." As we talked he told me of numerous pictures they had obtained. Finally, he said they had taken the picture of Jesus giving the Sermon on the Mount. When he contended that *he did not know who it was because the man speaking did not resemble Di Vinci's painting of the Christ,* the sum total of all the questions I had intended to ask him was answered. How could he possibly live with Jesus for months on end and not know what He looked like? Doug DeVorss heard Spalding make this statement and Doug knew it freed me from any and all illusions about the Spalding books. This information, no doubt, contributed to Doug's idea that he must not let me find out more about Spalding and, above all, put it into a book.

In months to come, I heard Spalding make the same statement in public in regard to not knowing Jesus' photograph because He did not resemble Di Vinci's painting of Him. One man in the audience asked Spalding why he would not recognize the picture of Jesus after all the time he spent with Him. Baird suddenly became a little deaf, confused the issue and never did answer the man's question. This happened in Los Angeles and scores of people who read this will remember the occasion of which I speak.

When Baird admitted he did not know the picture of Jesus he, at the same time, denied the existence of a Time Camera. Had there actually been a Time Camera which caught a picture of the great Master, Spalding would have never relaxed until he authenticated it beyond doubt. His whole life had been regarded with suspicion by perhaps as many people as those who believed his story. I have reason to think he would have devoted his last ounce of strength to prove just one of his erratic assertions.

I was finally successful in establishing what seems

logical to believe as his correct birthplace and birthdate. Apparently, he was born in Kohocton, New York on May 26, 1872.

A natural question is, how do I account for his saying he was 95 years old in the telekenesis contact? This was probably an impression he carried with him and his answer was a matter of reflex rather than based on thought. In this same contact, he urged me to stress his great love for humanity. This is in line with the desire for adoration which he carried into the astral plane with him and it seems only natural that he would like to enjoy that emotional stimulus from this plane. I cannot conscientiously stress that he had any love for humanity not common to the average person living in a confused state of mind. I might point out that if he had felt such a great love for humanity while he was on earth he would have done something about it. As I knew him, he made no contributions either in money or service toward a single philanthropic enterprise of any kind. On the contrary, I do know he was very earnest in his solicitations of funds, over a long period of years, for his own ventures, principally mining and oil. It may be argued he intended to turn over his profits to a worthy cause but, if he never paid income tax, his inclinations to keep his money are fairly well established. He did not even belong to a service club. So far as his learning the lesson of tolerance, as his greatest lesson in life, it is a well-proven fact from the most ancient teachings that one learns tolerance as he eliminates the nonconductors of Self expression from his life; then, tolerance is the lesson each individual learns because of his tolerance with himself, not with others, first.

Perhaps the most difficult lesson to learn is self-tolerance. This means that one must strike a mental balance within himself which will allow him to observe and appraise his acts devoid of emotionalism. The sincere student should strive to review his actions without condemning himself and thereby stifling his progress and without condoning or justifying his acts and thus providing subtle avenues of escape. When one ceases to blame another for his own thoughts and, at the same time, takes definite measures to bring his thinking into alignment with his purpose in living, he can be assured that the remainder of the Path will unfold ahead of him. Spalding's reactions to Life were not founded on reason or logic or clarity of thought; they were strictly emotional and according to his desires.

Baird T. Spalding was very sensitive to the thoughts of his public and to what they expected of him. He knew they regarded him as embodying a great love for humanity and tolerance. As long as he remains a dweller on the astral planes, companioned by his "controls," whatever earth-plane contacts he makes will be consistent with ideas he held while in a physical body. Discarnate souls are on the desire plane because of their own desire. It is well nigh impossible to receive reliable information from them; but, while trying, one might easily become involved with an astral entity himself. It should be remembered that they are not so interested in promoting high ideals on the earth as they are in finding a physical means to gratifying desire. I speak here of only a portion of souls occupying astral realms. By no means are all of them working for the downfall of humanity. Just a certain band of astral entities comprise a type whose chief interest lies in obsessing physical bodies.

A concentrated effort was once made to deify Baird Spalding. Even if he had enacted the evolvement attributed to him by his admirers, they would not have benefitted by his deification. Other than personal glory, there could have been no object in Spalding permitting this to happen. Were he expanded to meet the most fanciful dreams of his, he would have been, at best, a conveyor of a message. He was not the message itself. One would not think of showering adoration on a Western Union boy at the sacrifice of the message he was delivering! Jesus taught, "I of myself am nothing . . ." and directed attention to the Principle within.

Baird T. Spalding *As I Knew Him*

Our civilization, or lack of it, has pyramided to a point where mankind, in the individual units, must adhere to Principle in directing his affairs. The only alternative he has is self destruction.

No writing on Baird Spalding's life would be complete if a discussion of his books was ignored. I feel that the time has come when the mystery of the Spalding books can be revealed. In advance, I wish to state that I have checked and double-checked this story and have fitted together pieces of conversation that I have had with both Douglas K. DeVorss and Baird T. Spalding until I am satisfied that it is authentic. Besides I have confirmed my findings with people who knew Spalding before his first book was published.

As I have previously mentioned, John Spalding, grandfather of Baird T. Spalding, lived the greater part of his life in India. He was a devout follower of the Hindu teachings. He traveled extensively through the Himalayan mountains and was a frequent visitor to numerous Ashrams. It is said that John Spalding made many contacts with the Masters. Whether these "Masters" were Temple Priests, heads of Ashrams or Those who had won Their liberation is something I was unable to ascertain. All evidence points to Their being "genuine" Masters, though.

CONCLUSION

One of the Masters had written a manuscript in which He disclosed intimate details of Their daily lives, some clarification on religious thought and general information which They wished printed and made available for public consumption. They hoped to stimulate a fresh interest among seekers of Truth that would elevate the individual's consciousness into a new concept of himself in relation to Life. They presented Mastership as the inevitable attainment for each human being. The writing was so designed that it would promote an expansion in consciousness for all who read it.

The Masters' manuscript was entrusted to John Spalding for publication but, for some reason unknown to me, he did not carry out his assignment. At John Spalding's death, the valuable writing fell into the hands of Baird T. Spalding. The story continues that Baird carried the handwritten manuscript with him for a number of years. He often read it to groups who were interested. Finally, a wealthy lady in Northern California saw the manuscript and asked Spalding if she could have 1,000 copies of it printed and distributed as gifts to her friends. He consented and the first printing took place in this manner. The demand for these books was unbelievable; consequently, when they were offered for sale more than 20,000 copies sold during the first three months.

The manuscript which was printed was in Baird Spalding's handwriting. After the original manuscript came into his possession Baird conceived the idea to re-work it. It was Baird Spalding's imagination that rearranged incidents to fit the needs of an "expedition" in which he played a major role. He changed it in many ways to make the original story more dramatic and spectacular. Baird referred to this writing as "The Book of Gold" and expected to make a fortune from it. Volume One of the Four Volumes of Spalding's writings contains what is left of the original Masters' manuscript.

Needless to say, the Masters' work was badly mutilated; nevertheless, a thread of authenticity ran through Spalding's version and Their purpose was accomplished to a large degree. The "Spalding Books" have led millions of people, all over the world, into a higher consciousness than any books written during the past two hundred years.

When Volume One swept the country like a prairie fire and Spalding was deluged by people asking for more of his "report" on the Masters, it put him in quite a spot. He was a famous man almost overnight with absolutely nothing to substantiate a single statement he had declared to be an actual experience. He was not a world traveler, scientist or even highly schooled. After two years, enough pressure was brought to bear on Spalding that he was forced to either render more of his "report" or admit that he was not the author. He took a chance on the former and scurried around to find bits of information that would continue the same trend of thoughts as Volume One and, assisted by the astral control, Volume Two was assembled.

Three supposedly authentic statements have been given me in regard to where the Third Volume was written. The first one maintained it was written in an apartment in Los Angeles; Doug DeVorss said it was written in the cabin of the late Dr. Mesik near San Diego and that it was taken from notes Baird made while in India. However, the third report was given to me by a reliable lady who said she typed the manuscript for Baird in her own home. Later, it was discovered that in the main it was plagiarized while the rest of it was taken from the magazine section of the Sunday papers. A plagiary suit was considered by the Hindu author whose material Baird stole. The Hindu finally decided to let the Great Law take care of the matter; besides, he learned that Baird had no money.

In the intervening years, between the publication of Volumes Two and Three, Baird T. Spalding lived a very hectic life. His affairs were so mixed up when DeVorss bought the Spalding publication in 1935 that a corps of five attorneys worked several weeks to get them in order.

Baird T. Spalding *As I Knew Him*

At the time the Third Volume was written Spalding was not living in ideal circumstances and, it is possibly conceivable, under the pressure, why he might plagiarize it or look over the Sunday papers for ideas, or both.

In fairness to Doug DeVorss, I should mention that when he signed Spalding to publish his books he urged Baird to "give credit where credit was due" for his writings. I suppose Spalding thought he was in too deep to do this because he refused. This may account for Doug's apprehension about my writing the Spalding story for, in a sense, DeVorss and Spalding had a pact of secrecy together.

My files contain many letters attesting to the fact that Spalding's books did achieve a purpose somewhat along the lines of the original motive behind them. Scores of people have told me that their first expansion of consciousness took place while they were reading a Spalding book. Many of them claim they have become clairaudient or clairvoyant, or both, while reading or shortly afterwards. Some say they have even understood the riddle of the universe for a brief second.

Just recently a man told me of an unusual experience which happened to him while he was earnestly studying Spalding's First Volume. He said, in reading, he had attained a blissful attitude toward life and wished to retire for the night in that particular state. Before going to sleep he heard beautiful poetry of words and phrases with which he was unfamiliar. After listening for a few minutes, he demanded to know the source of such beauty and instantly a robed figure appeared before him. Neither of them spoke but the figure remained for about five minutes and was visible with the man's eyes open or closed.

Another person wrote to me that he opened the door to a darkened room in his house after reading a Spalding book, and the room flooded with a soft, white light.

Others declare as they read the books, geometric figures appear in light upon the page. Some say the books have turned to light in their hands.

Numerous other persons have related to me how they were whisked out of their bodies and placed in strange settings where they have witnessed ceremonies, et cetera.

To me, the most interesting thing about Baird T. Spalding, as I knew him, was the fact that if he had been any different than he was, the success of his books would have been hindered. It seems they had to be put across by a man whom science would ignore and religion would not challenge. He never defended anything he said and I never knew him to attempt proof of his statements. People accepted him whole-heartedly because he told them what they wanted to hear. In other words, something about his books confirmed an inner conviction each one feels about his ability to attain spiritual understanding. His writings gave people a release from the hell and damnation of Christianity and, above all, rescued them from being classified as sinners living in a veil of tears.

A prominent judge once jokingly remarked to Spalding, "Why, Baird, if what you say of the Masters in India is true, every news agency in the world would rush reporters and cameramen there to verify your story."

"No they wouldn't," replied Baird

"Why not?" questioned the judge.

"Because they don't believe me," answered Spalding

And this, I think is the secret of success for the Spaldings books. People who were in a position to interfere with their circulation did not believe them; therefore, they were unhampered in reaching the multitudes who would believe them.

It may be understood now what I mean in saying that I do not consider that Baird T. Spalding was a great man; rather, he was fabulous and fantastic and he did fulfill a great destiny in a fantastic way. His books, whether garbled or not have ushered in the New Age of Light.

THE END

ABOUT THE AUTHOR . . .

David Bruton's training in esoteric studies began at an early age, and he developed extraordinary powers of discernment in the values of life, together with an unusual ability to transmit his learning to others. After a successful career in music, he gained a fine reputation as a doctor during ten years of practice. He was Founder-President of the Institute of Esoteric Philosophy, a non-profit organization devoted to the dissemination of the psychologically sound and realistic way of life taught by the Masters of all religions. His earlier book, *The Unknown God Revealed*, is now out of print.

Mr. Bruton knew Baird T. Spalding well over a period of years. He conducted his funeral service and administered his estate.

THE LIFE AND TEACHING
OF THE
MASTERS OF THE FAR EAST

by BAIRD T. SPALDING

Baird T. Spalding, whose name became legend in metaphysical and truth circles during the first half of the 20th century, played an important part in introducing to the Western world the knowledge that there are Masters, or Elder Brothers, who are assisting and guiding the destiny of mankind. The countless numbers of letters that have come in through the years, from all over the world, bear testimony of the tremendous help received from the message in these books.

Partial listing of the contents of the five volumes:

Volume I: Introduction of the Master Emil—Visit to the "Temple of Silence"—Astral projection—Walking on Water—Visit to the Healing Temple—Emil talks about America—The Snowmen of the Himalayas—New Light on the teachings of Jesus.

Volume II: Visit to the Temple of the Great Tau Cross—Visit with the Master Jesus—Jesus discusses the nature of hell; the nature of God—The Mystery of thought vibrations—Jesus feeds the multitude—An account of a healing experience—Jesus and Buddha visit the group.

Volume III: One of the masters speaks of the Christ consciousness—The nature of cosmic energy—The creation of the planets and the worlds—The trip to Lhasa—Visit at the Temple Pora-tat-sanga—Explaining the mystery of levitation—A doubter becomes convinced of the existence of Jesus.

Volume IV: This material was first presented as "The India Tour Lessons." Each chapter has text for study, as well as guides to teachers for developing and interpreting the material. Among subjects covered: The White Brotherhood—The One Mind—Basis of coming social reorganization—Prana.

Volume V: Material taken from lectures given by Mr. Spalding in California during the last two years of his life. There is also a brief biographical sketch. Partial contents: Camera of past events—Is there a God—The divine pattern—The reality—Mastery over death—The law of supply.

Each of the 5 volumes has approximately 175 pages.